N

A
Comparable Worth
Primer

A
Comparable Worth
Primer

Steven L. Willborn
University of Nebraska

Lexington Books
D.C. Heath and Company/Lexington, Massachusetts/Toronto

Library of Congress Cataloging in Publication Data

Willborn, Steven L.
  A comparable worth primer.

  Bibliography: p.
  Includes index.
  1. Equal pay for equal work—Law and legislation—United States. 2. Women—Wages—
Law and legislation—United States. 3. Sex discrimination in employment—Law and
legislation—United States. 4. Equal pay for equal work—United States. 5. Women—
Wages—United States. 6. Sex discrimination in employment—United States. I. Title.
KF3467.W55 1986   344.73′0121   85-40329
ISBN 0-669-11018-3 (alk. paper)   347.304121

Published simultaneously in Canada
Printed in the United States of America on acid-free paper
Casebound International Standard Book Number: 0-669-11018-3
Library of Congress Catalog Card Number: 85-40329

The paper used in this publication meets the minimum requirements of American National
Standard for Information Sciences—Permanence of Paper for Printed Library Materials,
ANSI Z39.48-1984.

∞™

The last numbers on the right below indicate the number and date of printing.

10 9 8 7 6 5 4 3 2 1

95 94 93 92 91 90 89 88 87 86

To Elizabeth

Contents

Figures and Tables

Acknowledgments

A cknowledgments for this book come under three headings: people, money, and libraries. I must thank Elizabeth Hazen Willborn for reviewing drafts and general encouragement and support; Benjamin J. Eicher and Mary E. Haberland for research assistance on state legislation; Pat Knapp, Timothy Loudon, and Marilyn McNabb for reviewing drafts; Marie Wiechman for library assistance; Linda Bankson for overseas liaison; and Barb Homer for secretarial assistance.

Research for the book was made possible through financial assistance provided by the Fulbright Commission and by a Ross McCollum Summer Research Grant from the University of Nebraska Foundation.

Finally, I am grateful for the staffs and resources of the libraries where the research was conducted: University of Nebraska College of Law Library, Lincoln, Nebraska; University of Nebraska Love Library, Lincoln, Nebraska; Institute of Advanced Legal Studies Library, London; British Library, London; and University of London Library, London.

Introduction to Comparable Worth

C omparable worth has become a familiar term in legal and political debate. It refers to a discrimination theory, but it is also a rallying cry for activists, a slogan for politicians, and a litmus test for both liberals and conservatives. It has been called the women's issue of the 1980s and the feminist road to socialism. But despite its wide usage, the term has been used with great imprecision and is more often misunderstood than understood. One must begin, then, by examining the historical antecedents of comparable worth, by articulating a comparable worth theory and by contrasting this theory with the common understanding of comparable worth.

Women have always been paid less than men. Although the disparity has been greater, since the 1930s women have consistently earned about 60 percent of what men have earned. (Male-female wage disparities are discussed in more detail in Chapter 1.) Until the 1960s, it seemed obvious that sex discrimination was largely responsible for this. It was a common practice for employers to pay women less than men even if they were doing the same work. The practice was often justified by the dubious proposition that men required higher wages because they supported families, but women did not. In the 1960s, legislatures began to address the male-female wage disparity by enacting statutes that required equal pay for equal work. Thus, if men and women were doing the same work, the federal Equal Pay Act of 1963* and its many state clones required employers to pay them equally. Ironically, the equal pay acts, rather than correcting the male-female wage disparity, merely highlighted the subtlety of the problem. The equal pay acts are now almost universally observed and women generally receive the same pay as men doing the same work. Nevertheless, women continue to earn, on average, about 60 percent of what men earn. Why? Because unequal pay for equal work was not the principal cause of the male-female wage disparity. Other more complex factors were at work.

Comparable worth is the logical outgrowth of the promise and limita-

---

*29 U.S.C. sec. 206(d) (1982).

tions of the equal pay efforts of the 1960s and 1970s. The equal pay acts promised to address the male-female wage gap, but they proved to be inadequate to the task. The equal pay acts could only have been effective if they were right about the cause of the wage disparity. Unfortunately, experience proved that they were not. The comparable worth movement shifted the focus to another possible explanation for the wage gap—job segregation. Perhaps there is a wage gap because women perform different, and lower paying, jobs than men. And perhaps the jobs women perform are lower paying because women do them. If that is the case, the wage gap may be the result of a form of sex discrimination that the equal pay acts did not address—sex discrimination in the setting of wages for female-dominated occupations. This contention forms the heart of comparable worth and provides the seed for the development of a comparable worth theory.

As the preceding historical survey would suggest, the theory of comparable worth contains factual and legal propositions. The factual proposition is that the compensation rates for occupations are affected by the sex composition of the occupation. In the cases that have arisen to date, the claim has been that the compensation rates for jobs occupied predominately by women are lower than they would be if the jobs were not sex dominated. Thus, nurses might claim that they would be paid more if the occupation, instead of being female dominated, contained equal numbers of men and women. The legal proposition is that the effect of sex composition on compensation rates is sex discrimination and is, therefore, prohibited by the employment discrimination laws. The difference between what occupations are paid and what they would be paid if sex composition did not influence the compensation rate is the extent of the sex discrimination. Thus, if nurses are paid x as a female-dominated occupation, but would be paid $x + y$ as an occupation that contained an equal number of men and women, y is the extent of the sex discrimination.

Even this broad articulation of the theory begins to focus the comparable worth debate. First, comparable worth applies only to wage rates. It does not apply to other types of employment conditions such as hiring, promotion, or discharge practices. Thus, comparable worth theory might be used to raise the wages of a female-dominated occupation, but it would not be used to alter hiring practices. Second, although comparable worth is generally considered to be a women's issue, many men would benefit if the theory were accepted. Comparable worth affects not the wage rates of women, but the wage rates of occupations. As a result, if comparable worth were accepted as a theory and used to increase the wage rates of a female-dominated occupation, the benefited class would be the incumbents of that occupation, both male and female. Third, although the theory is clearly capable of broader application, it has only been applied to increase the compensation of female-dominated occupations. If an occupation contains a relatively equal number of male and female incumbents, the effect of sex composition on wage rates, which is the heart of comparable worth theory, is obscured. One would guess that the theory could be applied to reduce the compensation of male-dominated occupations, but no cases to date have broached the subject.

Although pay equity is a term that is sometimes used interchangeably with comparable worth, the two terms are distinct. The term comparable worth, properly used, refers only to the effect of an occupation's sex composition on the compensation of that occupation. Pay equity refers to any wage disparities that might be considered inequitable. Thus, if the claim were made that the compensation of nurses was unfair because they were paid less than secretaries even though nursing required greater skill, effort, and responsibility, pay equity would be the issue. It seems inequitable that nurses should be paid less in those circumstances. Comparable worth would not be an issue because, since both occupations are female dominated, there is no claim that this disparity is caused by the sex composition of the occupations. Comparable worth, then, is one type of pay equity issue.

The common understanding of comparable worth, including that of the majority of scholarly work in the area, is that comparable worth requires equal pay for work that is of comparable value to the employer. Value to the employer is defined in terms of the skill, effort, and responsibility required to do the job. Thus, if an employer employs janitors and secretaries and the two jobs, although different, require equal amounts of skill, effort, and responsibility, the employer, according to this understanding of comparable worth, should be required to pay the jobs equally. But that is a pay equity notion; it seems inequitable to differentially compensate two jobs that require equal amounts of skill, effort, and responsibility. Comparable worth asks additional questions: Is the pay disparity the result of sex discrimination? Or, more narrowly, are secretaries paid less than they would be if most of them were not women or are janitors paid more than they would be if most of them were not men? If the disparity is the result of sex discrimination, comparable worth requires that the jobs be paid equally. If the disparity is not the result of discrimination, comparable worth notions are irrelevant to the disparity. Thus, theoretically, instead of comparing janitors to secretaries, comparable worth compares the wages of the secretary job as a sex-dominated occupation to the wages the job would be paid if it were not sex dominated. If there is a disparity between what the secretaries are paid and what they would be paid if the job were not sex dominated, the difference is attributable to the sex of the incumbents and, hence, is illegal.

The common understanding of comparable worth comes from comparable worth litigation. In litigation, plaintiffs have presented evidence that: (1) women occupying a female-dominated occupation (secretaries) (2) are paid less than (3) men occupying a male-dominated occupation (janitors) (4) for work that is comparable in skill, effort, and responsibility. Plaintiffs have then argued that this evidence creates an inference of illegal sex discrimination. (Legal analysis of comparable worth claims is discussed in chapter 2.) This makes sense in the context of litigation where decisions must be made on the basis of incomplete information and in the face of uncertainty. If we cannot know with certainty whether secretaries would be paid more if the occupation were not female dominated, perhaps we should create an inference of sex discrimination if there is a wage disparity between secretaries and janitors. This should not, however, affect comparable worth theory. The relevant comparison is between the wages of secretaries as members of a female-dominated occupation and the wages of secretaries as members of a sex-neutral occupation. The comparison between secretaries and janitors is used because the information is readily available and because it is of inferential value in making the relevant comparison.

Comparable worth analysis under this theory requires a type of mysticism. Mysticism, or something very much like it, is required to know with any degree of certainty what secretaries would be paid if the occupation were not female dominated. Despite this mysticism, comparable worth theory should not be thought of as a departure from traditional discrimination theory. Traditional theory requires the same type of mysticism. In the traditional case, a woman applies for a job and is not hired. To prevail on a discrimination charge, the woman must prove that she would have been hired if she were male. But, of course, she is not male, so she must attempt to create an inference of discrimination. Usually she does this by comparing herself to a similarly situated male, for example, to the male who applied for the same job and was hired. If she can prove, for example, that she is more qualified than the male who was hired, the inference is that she was not hired because of her sex. Comparable worth theory applies to groups rather than individuals, but it perfectly mirrors the traditional analysis. Secretaries, for example, must prove that they would be paid more if the occupation were not female dominated. But, of course, the occupation is female dominated, so the secretaries must attempt to create an inference of discrimination. Usually they do this by comparing themselves to a similarly situated occupation, for example, to janitors who work for the same employer and whose job requires equal or lesser amounts of skill, effort, and responsibility. If secretaries can prove their case, the inference is that secretaries would be paid more if not for the sex of the majority of the incumbents. Thus, comparable worth is merely an application of traditional theory to a group setting and, more specifically, to the wage-setting process for occupations.

A frequently repeated objection to comparable worth is that it is impossible to compare the value of two different jobs without reference to the market. Even if the secretary and janitor jobs require equal amounts of skill, effort, and responsibility (and that judgment, by itself, is very difficult and subjective), a number of other factors, such as the number of persons willing to work as secretaries or janitors and the number of positions available, may affect the value of the jobs to an employer. (Methods of evaluating and comparing jobs are discussed in chapter 3.) A proper comparable worth theory overcomes this objection. In theory, secretaries are not compared to janitors. In theory, the secretarial job classification is compared to the same job classification with every market condition exactly the same except that the classification is no longer dominated by females. Thus, there is no need to compare the "value" of different jobs. Comparable worth, instead, compares the wages of the same job as a sex-segregated occupation and as a sex-neutral occupation.

Comparable worth, though, is much more than a theory. It is an attempt through economic and legal means to change the historical relationship between male and female wages. Chapter 1 discusses the economics of comparable worth. Comparable worth will succeed in closing the male-female wage gap only if its underlying assumption—that the gap is caused primarily by the undercompensation of female-dominated work—is true. Economic analysis provides us with a framework to assess this assumption. Economics also provides us with an avenue for putting comparable worth theory into practice; it provides us with one means of measuring the alleged undercompensation of women's work. Finally, economics allows us to assess the side effects of comparable worth—will it lead to inflation, unemployment, and a host of other ills? The rest of the book discusses comparable worth as a legal phenomenon. Chapter 2 examines the developing federal law on the topic and chapter 3 outlines the burgeoning and varied state responses to the issue. Chapter 4 considers comparable worth as an international phenomenon. Virtually every major industrialized country has dealt with the comparable worth issue in one fashion or another. The experiences of other countries should help us evaluate the response of this country to the issue.

This book will not tell you whether comparable worth is good or bad. That is a decision for you to make. The book will provide you with a broader base of information on which to make your decision. And your decision is important because in a democracy it is your decision, and the decisions of your fellow citizens, that will decide the still-uncertain fate of comparable worth.

1
The Economics of Comparable Worth

E conomics is at the heart of the comparable worth debate. Comparable worth theory is designed to eliminate wage disparities between men and women that are caused by discrimination. Economic analysis allows us to measure and assess these wage disparities and provides us with tools to address the issue of whether the wage disparities are caused by discrimination. The first section of this chapter analyzes male-female wage disparities and explores the discrimination issue. Economic analysis also enables us to assess the probable economic consequences if comparable worth is implemented. What will it cost? Who will pay? The second section of this chapter examines these economic consequences.

Wage Disparities and Sex Discrimination

There is a significant wage disparity between the earnings of women as a group and the earnings of men as a group. The average working women earns about 60 percent of what the average working man earns. The disparity displays a stubborn persistency over time and within age groups. The disparity and its persistency are important because they help to explain the existence of comparable worth and the controversy surrounding it.

In 1981, a working woman earned 59.2 percent of what a working man earned. The median income of women who worked full time in year-round jobs was $12,001. The median income of men who worked full time in year-round jobs was $20,260.[1] As one would expect, women were overrepresented among workers whose earnings were low and underrepresented among workers whose earnings were high. Sixty-four percent of all workers who earned $7,000 to $10,000 were women, while only 3 percent of all workers who earned over $75,000 were women. (See table 1–1.)

1981 was not an unusual year. As illustrated by figure 1–1, the earnings disparity between men and women has remained relatively constant for at least the last thirty years. But, the earnings gap is even more persistent than

Table 1–1
Women as a Percentage of All Earners, by Earnings Group, 1981
(persons 15 years of age and over)

Earnings Group	Number (in thousands)		Distribution (percent)		Women as Percent of All Earners
	Women	Men	Women	Men	
Total	23,329	41,773	100.0	100.0	35.8
Less than $3,000	537	1,031	2.3	2.5	34.2
$3,000–$4,999	594	465	2.5	1.1	56.1
$5,000–$6,999	1,601	1,137	6.9	2.7	58.5
$7,000–$9,999	4,736	2,713	20.3	6.5	63.6
$10,000–$14,999	8,186	7,438	35.1	17.8	52.4
$15,000–$24,999	6,452	15,013	27.7	35.9	30.1
$25,000–$49,999	1,170	12,005	5.0	28.7	8.9
$50,000–$74,999	32	1,347	0.1	3.2	2.3
$75,000 and over	21	625	0.1	1.5	3.3

Source: Adapted from U.S. Department of Labor, *Time of Change: 1983 Handbook on Women Workers* (Washington, D.C.: U.S. Government Printing Office, 1983), 83.

figure 1–1 would indicate. The gap existed long before 1955. Although it probably existed even earlier, the gap can first be documented in this country in 1815, when the earnings of women in agriculture were 28.8 percent of the earnings of men in agriculture. As industrialization spread, the earnings gap narrowed until about 1930, when the gap reached its present level of about 60 percent.[2] Although some predict the earnings gap to narrow by the year 2000, no one expects it to disappear in the forseeable future.[3]

The earnings gap exists at every age level. (See table 1–2.) The earnings gap for young workers is relatively small, but the gap steadily grows until, presumably, high-income men begin to retire or die. The reason for the growth in the gap is that male incomes go up with age until retirement, while female incomes remain static. There is little change in female income from the 25 to 34 years age bracket to the 55 to 64 years age bracket.

The existence of wage disparities, however, does not necessarily mean that comparable worth adjustments should be made. Comparable worth theory requires adjustments only if the disparities are caused by sex discrimination. If the disparities are caused by other factors, they do not violate comparable worth notions. The relevant question, then, is what is the cause of these disparities? Economics offers two types of analysis to address this question. The first focuses on differences between male and female workers and the second on differences between male and female jobs.

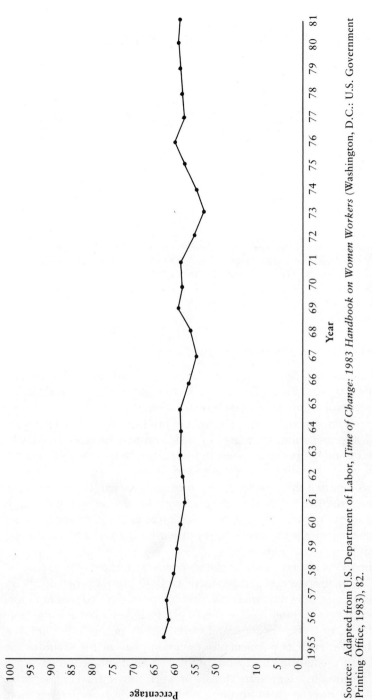

Source: Adapted from U.S. Department of Labor, *Time of Change: 1983 Handbook on Women Workers* (Washington, D.C.: U.S. Government Printing Office, 1983), 82.

Note: For 1967–1981, earnings include wage and salary income and earnings from self-employment; for 1955–1966, earnings include wage and salary income only. For 1979–1981, data are for persons fifteen years of age and over; for 1955–1978, data are for persons fourteen years of age and over.

Figure 1–1. Women's Earnings as a Percentage of Men's Earnings, 1955–1981

Table 1–2
Annual Median Income in 1981 of Year-Round Full-Time Workers, by Age and Sex

| | Income | | Women's Income as |
Age[a]	Women	Men	a Percent of Men's
Total	$12,457	$20,692	60.2
15–19 years	7,598	8,252	92.1
20–24 years	10,173	12,408	82.0
25–34 years	13,377	19,185	69.7
35–44 years	13,552	23,368	58.0
45–54 years	12,784	24,096	53.1
55–64 years	12,903	23,013	56.1
65 years and older	14,487	20,647	70.2

Source: U.S. Department of Labor, *Time of Change: 1983 Handbook on Women Workers* (Washington, D.C.: U.S. Government Printing Office, 1983), 96.
[a]As of March 1982.

The Wage Disparity and Worker Characteristics

Gary Becker has used neoclassical economic theory to define discrimination as decisions that are made on the basis of factors other than productivity.[4] In setting wages, for example, an employer discriminates if he pays different wages to males and females who are equally productive. Conversely, in the absence of discrimination, the wages of male and females who are equally productive should be the same. Thus, in theory, one should be able to determine if the wage disparity between men and women is caused by discrimination by comparing the productivity of men and women. If men are sufficiently more productive than women to account for the wage disparity, it is not the result of discrimination. If, however, productivity differences do not account for the entire wage disparity, the disparity that is not accounted for is attributable to discrimination.

The theory, as always, is easier stated than implemented. The theory requires one to quantify wages and productivity. Both present problems. Wage data, in most cases, does not reflect the total compensation received for a job. The income figures in table 1–2, for example, include money income from wages, salaries, tips, commissions, and so on, but do not include employer-provided benefits such as payments to a pension plan, or for health or life insurance, or for educational expenses. Other types of compensation—such as a work location in a temperate climate or work-related travel to desirable locations—also present quantification problems. Productivity is even more difficult to quantify. Researchers who have attempted to quantify it have acknowledged the limitations of their efforts.[5] Instead of attempting to measure productivity directly, then, researchers have attempted to measure it indirectly by using worker characteristics such as education, health, and experience as proxies for productivity. As a result, in practice the research has compared male and female wages to the characteristics of male and female workers. To the extent worker characteristics do not account for wage differentials, the residual wage differential is attributed to discrimination.

This research approach is based on "human capital" theory.[6] Under this theory, workers invest in their earnings power or human capital by acquiring those characteristics that are valued in the labor market, just as other entrepreneurs might invest in a machine or factory. Workers then seek the highest return available on their investments. If the market were perfect, male and female returns on human capital should equalize.[7] Differences in male and female returns must reflect market imperfections, discrimination or both.

The basic procedure in human capital studies is to estimate the expected earnings of one sex if that sex received return on human capital equal to the other sex and to compare those expected earnings to that sex's actual earnings. To illustrate, assume that the only worker characteristics valued in the market are years of schooling and years of work experience.[8] The researcher would first determine the effect of each characteristic on male earnings by using a statistical technique known as multiple regression analysis. Assume that the regression analysis yields the following information for males:

$$\text{Earnings} = \$1,000 + \$500(\text{schooling}) + \$200(\text{experience})$$

If the average amount of schooling for males is ten years and the average years of experience for males is twenty years, the average earnings for males would be $10,000: $1,000 + $500(10) + $200(20). Now assume that the average level of earnings for women is $6,000, that their average amount of schooling is eleven years, and that they have an average of ten years of work experience. The researcher would next determine the expected earnings of females if there were an equal return on human capital by substituting the average work characteristics of women into the earnings equation for men. Thus, the expected earnings equation for women would be as follows:

$$\text{Earnings} = \$1,000 + \$500(11) + \$200(10) = \$8,500$$

Thus, the gross earnings gap between males and females in this example is $4,000. But about one-third of the gap ($10,000 − $8,500 = $1,500) is attributable to human capital differences between men and women—in this example to differences in education and experience. The other two-thirds of the gap ($8,500 − $6,000 = $2,500) is attributable to differences in the return males and females receive on their human capital. In this type of study, differences in return are generally interpreted to represent discrimination.

In the human capital studies that have been done, worker characteristics account for only a small portion of the earnings difference between men and women. Table 1–3 summarizes the findings of several of these studies. The studies that explain the largest portion of the gap explain only 42 to 45 percent of the earnings differential, and most of the studies explain a much smaller portion of the gap than that. Proponents of comparable worth attribute the unexplained portion of the gap to discrimination.

Human capital studies, however, do not definitively resolve the issue of whether wage disparities are caused by discrimination. The studies have a number of theoretical and practical limitations. First, Becker's theoretical definition of discrimination as non-productivity-based decisions is by no means universally accepted. In a perfectly competitive environment, nondiscriminatory firms would hire equally productive but cheaper employees than discriminatory firms and, hence, should be able to grow and eventually to force discriminatory firms out of the market.[9] But that, of course, has not happened and, as a result, Becker's theoretical model is clouded. In addition, many economic theorists argue that a number of factors other than productivity, such as custom and union strength, affect wages.[10] Consequently, a disparity between wages and productivity may not necessarily be an indication of discrimination.

The use of worker characteristics as proxies for productivity is another shortcoming of human capital studies. The studies assume that there is a direct relationship between the worker characteristics studied and productivity. If that is not the case, and some would dispute it, the studies tell us little about discrimination as defined by Becker.[11] Moreover, even if one accepts the relationship between worker characteristics and productivity, the measurement of worker characteristics in these studies is problematic. For example, even if one accepts that there is a direct relationship between education and productivity, is "years of education" a sufficiently accurate measure of education or should the researcher be required to consider and quantify the quality and type of education received?

A third set of concerns involves limitations of the multiple regression technique that is used to determine the effect of worker characteristics on earnings.[12] For the multiple regression analysis to be reliable, all worker characteristics that might affect earnings must be included in the analysis; the worker characteristics that are included in the analysis must be independent of each other; and the variance of the errors must not change systematically with the observations.[13] If all relevant worker characteristics are not included in the analysis, an undetermined portion of the unexplained wage gap may be attributable to the relevant worker characteristics omitted instead of to discrimination. If the worker characteristics included in the analysis are not

Table 1–3
Percentage of Male-Female Earnings Differential Explained by Worker Characteristics

Author and Reference No.	Data Base	Characteristics Studied	Earnings Ratios		Percentage of Gap Explained[a]
			Observed	Adjusted	
Blinder (1)	White persons, except household heads younger than age 25 and household heads who did not work for money, 1967	Age, region, parents' income, father's education, place of birth, number of siblings, health, local labor market conditions, geographic mobility, seasonal employment	.54	.54	0
Cohen (2)	Full-time workers aged 22–64, and self-employed with a steady job, who worked 35 hours or more per week, 1969	Hours worked, fringe benefits and absenteeism, seniority, education, unionization	.55	.74	42
Corcoran (3)	5,000 white male heads of households and wives, and female heads of households, 1976	Work history	.67	.76	36
Corcoran and Duncan (4)	Household heads and spouses, 1976	Work history, labor force attachment, education, size of city, region	.74	.85	44
Daymont and Andrisani (5)	National Longitudinal Studies of the high school class of 1972, 1979	Work experience, job preference in high school, college major, highest degree, family situation	.93	.96	44
Fuchs (6)	Nonfarm employed persons, 1960	Color, schooling, age, city size	.60	.61	3
		Color, schooling, age, city size, marital status, class of worker, length of commute	.60	.66	15

Table 1–3 continued

Author and Reference No.	Data Base	Characteristics Studied	Earnings Ratios		Percentage of Gap Explained[a]
			Observed	Adjusted	
Gwartney and Stroup (7)	Full-time year-round workers, 1969	Age, education	.56	.56	0
	Single, never married workers, 1959	Age, education, hours worked	.98	.93	—
	Married, spouse-present workers, 1959	Age, education, hours worked	.33	.51	27
Mellor (8)	Full-time wage and salary workers, 1982	Age	.65	.65	0
		Years of schooling		.64	—
		Hours worked		.68	9
Mincer and Polachek (9)	White married men and women aged 30–44, 1967	Education, experience, work history	.66	.81	45
Oaxaca (10)	Urban employees, age 16 and over, reporting an hourly wage, 1967	Experience, education, health, part-time, migration, marital status, children, city size, region	.65	.72	20
Ragan and Smith (11)	Workers employed with pay in certain manufacturing industries, 1969–1970	Education, experience, marital status, race, health, region, urban residence, federal worker, turnover rate	.71	.84	43
Rytina (12)	Wage and salary workers aged 25 and over, 1981	Occupational tenure	.66	.67	3
Sandell and Shapiro (13)	White married men and women aged 30–44, 1967	Education, experience, work history	.66	.74	23

| Sawhill (14) | Employed wage and salary workers, 1967 | Race, region, age, education, weeks worked per year, hours worked per week | .46 | .56 | 19 |
| Tsuchigane and Dodge (15) | Year-round workers, 1970 | Hours worked, education, job seniority, absenteeism | .54 | .68 | 30 |

Calculated as follows: [(Adjusted − Observed)/(1 − Observed)] × 100.

(1) Alan S. Blinder, "Wage Discrimination: Reduced Form and Structural Estimates," *Journal of Human Resources* 8 (fall 1973):436–55.

(2) Malcolm S. Cohen, "Sex Differences in Compensation," *Journal of Human Resources* 6 (fall 1971):434–47.

(3) Mary E. Corcoran, "Work Experience, Labor Force Withdrawals, and Women's Wages: Empirical Results Using the 1976 Panel of Income Dynamics." In Cynthia B. Lloyd, Emily S. Andrews, and Curtis L. Gilroy, eds., *Women in the Labor Market* (New York: Columbia University Press, 1979), 216–45.

(4) Mary Corcoran and Greg J. Duncan, "Work History, Labor Force Attachment, and Earnings Differences Between the Races and Sexes," *Journal of Human Resources* 14 (winter 1979):3–20.

(5) Thomas N. Daymont and Paul J. Andrisani, "Job Preferences, College Major, and the Gender Gap in Earnings," *Journal of Human Resources* 19 (summer 1984):408–28.

(6) Victor R. Fuchs, "Differences in Hourly Earnings Between Men and Women," *Monthly Labor Review* 94 (May 1971):9–15.

(7) James Gwartney and Richard Stroup, "Measurement of Employment Discrimination According to Sex," *Southern Economic Journal* 39 (April 1973):575–87.

(8) Earl F. Mellor, "Investigating the Differences in Weekly Earnings of Women and Men," *Monthly Labor Review* 107 (June 1984):17–28.

(9) Jacob Mincer and Solomon Polachek, "Family Investments in Human Capital: Earnings of Women," *Journal of Political Economy* 82 (March/April 1974):S76–S108.

(10) Ronald Oaxaca, "Male-Female Wage Differentials in Urban Labor Markets," *International Economic Review* 14 (Oct. 1973):693–709.

(11) James F. Ragan, Jr., and Sharon P. Smith, "The Impact of Differences in Turnover Rates on Male/Female Pay Differentials," *Journal of Human Resources* 16 (summer 1981):343–65.

(12) Nancy F. Rytina, "Tenure as a Factor in the Male-Female Earnings Gap," *Monthly Labor Review* 105 (April 1982):32–34.

(13) Steven H. Sandell and David Shapiro, "A Reexamination of the Evidence," *Journal of Human Resources* 8 (winter 1978):103–17.

(14) Isabel V. Sawhill, "The Economics of Discrimination Against Women: Some New Findings," *Journal of Human Resources* 8 (summer 1973):383–96.

(15) Robert Tsuchigane and Norton Dodge, *Economic Discrimination Against Women in the United States* (Lexington, Mass: D.C. Heath, 1974), 35–43.

independent (that is, if a change in one characteristic is correlated with a change in another characteristic), the results of the multiple regression analysis are simply unreliable. This type of problem is called multicollinearity. The regression analysis will also be unreliable if the variance of the errors changes systematically with the observations. For example, if salespersons are all initially hired at the same salary so that there is very little variance in salaries at that time but the salaries of experienced salespersons are established by performance so that there is a wide and ever-expanding variance in salaries as salespersons become more experienced, the results of a regression designed to predict salary based on years of experience are likely to be unreliable. This type of problem is called heteroscedasticity.[14]

Finally, some argue that human capital studies severely underestimate the effect of sex discrimination on wages. These studies explain male-female wage disparities only to the extent that women have less human capital than men. But why do women have less human capital than men? One explanation may be that women are afforded fewer opportunities to acquire human capital because of sex discrimination. Employers, for example, may be less willing to hire or to train women because they believe women have a lesser attachment to the labor force than men.[15] To the extent this is true, human capital studies underestimate the effect of sex discrimination on wages because the factors the studies use to explain wage disparities are themselves infected with discrimination.

In summary, the current research that focuses on worker characteristics has been able to explain a portion of the wage disparity between men and women. Women have less human capital than men and, as a result, one would expect them to be less productive and to have lower earnings. The studies cannot, however, explain most of the disparity and some would attribute the unexplained portion to sex discrimination. That conclusion, though, is subject to a number of uncertainties that result from theoretical and practical problems with the research models. Thus, the current research that focuses on worker characteristics, although suggestive, cannot definitively resolve the issue of whether male-female wage disparities are caused by discrimination.

The Wage Disparity and Occupational Segregation

A second group of studies have focused on occupational segregation as the explanation for male-female wage disparities. There is no question that there is a great deal of occupational sex segregation. But to what extent does this segregation explain the wage disparity between men and women? And is the occupational distribution of men and women suspect as an explanation because it is, itself, a product of sex discrimination?

There is a considerable degree of occupational segregation, regardless of

Table 1–4
Occupational Segregation by Broad Occupational Grouping, 1981

Occupation	Total Employed (in thousands)	Women Employed (in thousands)	Women as Percentage of Total Employed
Private household workers	1,048	1,010	96.5
Health service workers	1,995	1,780	89.2
Clerical workers	18,564	14,938	80.5
Personal service workers	1,766	1,342	76.0
Service workers (except private household)	12,391	7,332	59.2
Sales workers	6,425	2,916	45.4
Professional and technical workers	16,419	7,319	44.6
Operatives	14,016	4,499	32.0
Managers and administrators	11,540	3,168	27.5
Farm laborers and supervisors	1,265	322	25.5
Nonfarm laborers	4,583	527	11.5
Farmers and farm managers	1,485	168	11.3
Craft and kindred workers	12,661	802	6.3

Source: Adapted from U.S. Department of Labor, *Time of Change: 1983 Handbook on Women Workers* (Washington, D.C.: U.S. Government Printing Office, 1983), 56.

how broadly or narrowly occupations are defined. Table 1–4 shows segregation within broadly defined occupational groupings. Women constitute 96.5 percent of private household workers and 89.2 percent of health service workers, but only 6.3 percent of craft and kindred workers and 11.5 percent of nonfarm laborers. Analysis of these broadly defined occupational groupings, however, may understate the extent of occupational segregation because there may be counterbalancing segregation within a broad grouping. The professional and technical workers grouping in table 1–4, for example, includes kindergarten teachers (98.4 percent female), registered nurses (96.8 percent female), engineering and science technicians (81.2 percent male), and physicians (86.3 percent male). As one would expect from this, analysis of narrower occupational groupings also discloses segregation. Of the 503 occupations included in the most disaggregated level of the 1980 census, more than 60 percent (324) had at least 70 percent male incumbents and another 12 percent (59) had at least 70 percent female incumbents. Fifty-six percent of the men and 26 percent of the women in the labor force were employed in occupations dominated by their own sex.[16] But these narrower occupational groupings may also underestimate the extent of segregation because there appears to be segregation within occupations. Several researchers have found

Table 1–5
Occupations with Highest and Lowest Mean Earnings, 1980

Ranking	Occupation	Percent Female	Mean Earnings
High			
1	Physicians	11	$57,166
2	Dentists	5	46,369
3	Lawyers	10	39,132
4	Podiatrists	5	38,402
5	Medical science teachers	17	37,958
6	Law teachers	13	36,411
7	Securities and financial services sales occupation	17	35,448
8	Airline pilots and navigators	1	34,488
9	Optometrists	6	34,211
10	Medical scientists	35	33,909
Low			
1	Child care workers, private household	98	$4,473
2	Private household cleaners and servants	92	5,530
3	Housekeepers and butlers	95	5,612
4	Child care workers, except private household	89	6,617
5	Cooks, private household	83	7,082
6	Waiters and waitresses	83	7,095
7	Miscellaneous food preparation occupations	56	7,548
8	Waiters and waitresses' assistants	46	7,623
9	Teachers' aides	88	7,628
10	Textile sewing machine operators	93	7,726

Source: Adapted from Bureau of the Census, *1980 Census of Population, vol. 2, Subject Reports, Earnings by Occupation and Education* (Washington, D.C.: U.S. Government Printing Office, 1984), 1–252.

that integrated occupations tend to be segregated by firm and that male-dominated firms tend to pay more than integrated firms, which tend to pay more than female-dominated firms.[17] There is no doubt, then, that there is significant occupational segregation by sex.

This occupational segregation clearly has some effect on the male-female wage gap because the work women do is generally paid less than the work men do. As indicated by table 1–5, only one of the ten top-paying professions included in the 1980 census has more than twenty percent female incumbents, while only two of the ten lowest-paying professions have less than eighty percent female incumbents.[18] As this would tend to indicate, the more an occupation is dominated by women, the less it pays. Figure 1–2 shows the

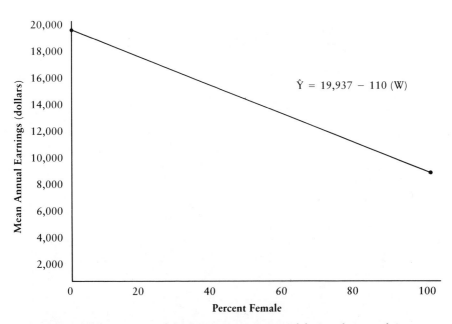

Source: Adapted from Bureau of the Census, *1980 Census of the Population, vol. 2, Subject Reports, Earnings by Occupation and Education* (Washington, D.C.: U.S. Government Printing Office, 1984), 1–252.

Notes: $\hat{Y}$ = estimated mean annual earnings and W = percent female in each occupation, $P < .0001$.

Based on data for 503 occupations included in the most detailed occupational breakdown of the 1980 census.

Figure 1–2. Relationship Between Percent Female and Mean Annual Earnings, 1980

relationship between the percentage of females in an occupation and the mean annual earnings of that occupation for both sexes. Each additional percent female in an occupation results in an average of $110 less in annual earnings. At the extremes, extremely female-dominated work is paid about $11,000 less annually than extremely male-dominated work.

Human capital studies, like those discussed in the previous section of this chapter, have been used to assess with more precision the effect of occupational segregation on the male-female wage disparity. These studies include occupation or occupational characteristics as one type of human capital that workers might possess.[19] Table 1–6 summarizes the findings of several of these studies.

The human capital studies that have included occupational characteris-

Table 1-6
Percentage of Male-Female Earnings Differential Explained by Occupational and Worker Characteristics

Author and Reference No.	Data Base	Characteristics Studied	Earnings Ratios		Percentage of Gap Explained[a]
			Observed	*Adjusted*	
General Studies					
Blinder (1)	White persons, except household heads younger than age 25 and household heads who did not work for money, 1967	Age, region, education, vocational training, occupation, union membership, veteran status, health, local labor conditions, geographical mobility, seasonal employment, length of time on job	.54	.70	35
Brown, et al. (2)	White males aged 45–59, 1966. White females aged 30–44 in 1967, 1971 data	Education, experience, part-time work, health, union membership, region, marital status, occupation	.62	.98	95
Featherman and Hauser (3)	Civilian noninstitutionalized men, married with spouse present, aged 20–64, and their wives, 1973	Education, occupation, hours worked, experience	.38	.48	16
Ferber and Spaeth (4)	Random sample of Illinois residents employed at least 20 hours per week on a single job	Experience, hours worked, education, marital status, industry, size of firm, supervisory authority, control over money, sex of supervisor	.49	.78	57
Filer (5)	Unique set developed by author from records of management consulting firm, 1967–1977	Race, age, military service, childhood environment, marital status, industry, education, intelligence, personality, values	.64	.77	37

Study	Sample	Controls			
Landes (6)	White persons, 14–65 years of age, employed in civilian labor force and not in school (within 96 occupations), 1967	Education, experience, hours worked, percent who worked full-time, percent who changed jobs since 1966, variance in weeks worked, differences in wages for experienced and inexperienced males, region	.71	.90	66
Mellor (7)	Full-time wage and salary workers, 1982	Occupation	.65	.70	14
		Industry	.65	.68	9
Oaxaca (8)	White urban employees, age 16 and over, reporting an hourly wage, 1967	Experience, education, class of worker, industry, occupation, health, part-time, migration, marital status, children, city size, region	.65	.78	37
Ragan and Smith (9)	Workers employed with pay in certain manufacturing industries, 1969–70	Education, experience, marital status, race, health, region, urban residence, federal worker, turnover rate, occupation	.71	.84	45
Roos (10)	Noninstitutionalized currently employed white workers aged 25–64, 1974, 1976, 1977	Age, education, hours worked, occupational characteristics, industry	.46	.63	32
Sanborn (11)	Employed civilian wage and salary earners, 1949	Occupation, hours of work, education, age, urban-rural status, race	.58	.76	43
		Above, but more narrowly defined occupations	.58	.82	57
		Above, plus turnover, absenteeism, work experience	.58	.88	71
Treiman and Hartmann (12)	Persons employed in occupations employing a minimum of 1,000 male and 1,000 female employees and reporting wage and salary earnings, 1970[b]	12 occupational groupings	.62	.63	3
		222 occupational groupings	.64	.68	11
		479 occupational groupings	.63	.70	35

Table 1–6 continued

Author and Reference No.	Data Base	Characteristics Studied	Earnings Ratios		Percentage of Gap Explained[a]
			Observed	Adjusted	
Treiman, Hartmann and Roos (13)	Census data for entire U.S. labor force, 1970	Education, experience, complexity of job, motor skills required by job, physical demands of job, working conditions	.57[c]	.83[c]	60
Studies in Specific Occupations					
Bayer and Astin (14)	Persons who received doctorate in natural science or social science between 1957 and 1962 who are employed full-time in academic settings, and whose primary work activity is teaching, 1964	Length of employment, type of employer, academic rank	.93	[d]	—
Gordon, Morton, and Braden (15)	1,000–2,000 academic employees of a large urban university	Age, seniority, race, education, rank, department	[e]	.89	—
Hirsch and Leppel (16)	487 full-time, tenure-track faculty of a state university, 1980–1981 academic year	Experience, rank, department, terminal degree, administrative appointment	.89	1.00	97
Johnson and Stafford (17)	Persons with Ph.D. degree in anthropology, biology, economics, mathematics, physics, and sociology, 1970	Experience, quality of graduate school, citizenship (by years since doctorate—in parenthesis) (0) (5) (15) (20) (25) (30)	.93 .88 .84 .82 .80 .79 .79	.93 .93 .93 .93 .93 .93 .93	0 42 55 62 65 67 67

Malkiel and Malkiel (18)	272 professional employees of a single corporation, 1969	Education, experience, publications, marital status, area of study, absence rate, job level	.65	.99	97
Remus and Kelley (19)	21–28-year-old graduates of the business school of a single university	Ethnicity, type of job, participation rate, college major	.81	.81	0

aCalculated as follows: [(Adjusted − Observed)/(1 − Observed)] × 100.

bThe study reports that it is based on 1970 census data at one point and on 1980 census data at another point. It is more likely that it was based on 1970 data.

cThis ratio is mean earnings of persons in female-dominated occupations to mean earnings of persons in male-dominated occupations instead of mean earnings of females to mean earnings of males.

dVaries from .84 to .99.

eNot reported.

(1) Alan S. Blinder, "Wage Discrimination: Reduced Form and Structural Estimates," *Journal of Human Resources* 8 (fall 1973):436–55.

(2) Randall S. Brown, Marilyn Moon, and Barbara S. Zoloth, "Incorporating Occupational Attainment in Studies of Male-Female Earnings Differentials," *Journal of Human Resources* 15 (winter 1980):3–28.

(3) David L. Featherman and Robert M. Hauser, "Sexual Inequalities and Socio-Economic Achievement in the U.S. 1967–1973," *American Sociological Review* 41 (June 1976):462–83.

(4) Marianne A. Ferber and Joe L. Spaeth, "Work Characteristics and the Male-Female Earnings Gap," *American Economic Review* 74 (May 1984):260–64.

(5) Randall K. Filer, "Sexual Differences in Earnings: The Role of Individual Personalities and Tastes," *Journal of Human Resources* 18 (winter 1983):82–99.

(6) Elizabeth M. Landes, "Sex-Differences in Wages and Employment: A Test of the Specific Capital Hypothesis," *Economic Inquiry* 15 (Oct. 1977):523–38.

(7) Earl F. Mellor, "Investigating the Differences in Weekly Earnings of Women and Men," *Monthly Labor Review* 107 (June 1984):17–28.

(8) Ronald Oaxaca, "Male-Female Wage Differentials in Urban Labor Markets," *International Economic Review* 14 (Oct. 1973):693–709.

(9) James F. Ragan, Jr., and Sharon P. Smith, "The Impact of Differences in Turnover Rates on Male/Female Pay Differentials," *Journal of Human Resources* 16 (summer 1981):343–65.

(10) Patricia A. Roos, "Sex Stratification in the Workplace: Male-Female Differences in Economic Returns to Occupation," *Social Science Research* 10 (March 1981):195–224.

Table 1–6 continued

(11) Henry Sanborn, "Pay Differences Between Men and Women," *Industrial and Labor Relations Review* 17 (July 1964):534–50.

(12) Donald J. Treiman and Heidi I. Hartmann, *Women, Work, and Wages: Equal Pay for Jobs of Equal Value* (Washington, D.C.: National Academy Press, 1981), 33–35.

(13) Donald J. Treiman, Heidi I. Hartmann, and Patricia A. Roos, "Assessing Pay Discrimination Using National Data," in Helen Remick, ed., *Comparable Worth and Wage Discrimination* (Philadelphia: Temple University Press, 1984), 137–49.

(14) Alan E. Bayer and Helen S. Astin, "Sex Differences in Academic Rank and Salary Among Science Doctorates in Teaching," *Journal of Human Resources* 3 (spring 1968):191–200.

(15) Nancy M. Gordon, Thomas E. Morton, and Ina C. Braden, "Faculty Salaries: Is There Discrimination by Sex, Race, and Discipline?" *American Economic Review* 64 (June 1974):419–27.

(16) Barry T. Hirsch and Karen Leppel, "Sex Discrimination in Faculty Salaries: Evidence from a Historically Women's University," *American Economic Review* 72 (Sept. 1982):829–35.

(17) George E. Johnson and Frank P. Stafford, "The Earnings and Promotion of Women Faculty," *American Economic Review* 64 (Dec. 1974):888–903.

(18) Burton G. Malkiel and Judith A. Malkiel, "Male-Female Pay Differentials in Professional Employment," *American Economic Review* 63 (Sept. 1973):693–705.

(19) William E. Remus and Lane Kelly, "Evidence of Sex Discrimination: In Similar Populations, Men Are Paid Better Than Women," *American Journal of Economics and Sociology* 42 (April 1983):149–52.

tics as an explanatory variable have generally explained more of the male-female wage disparity than the studies that have included only worker characteristics. But the results have not been uniform. Some studies have explained a large portion of the disparity, while others have explained even less than studies that included only worker characteristics.

As a general matter, however, the explanatory power of these studies increased as the occupations considered as variables became more narrowly defined. Treiman and Hartmann, for example, considered progressively more detailed occupational classifications. For 12 broadly defined classifications, occupation accounted for only 3 percent of the male-female wage disparity; for 222 classifications, occupation accounted for 11 percent of the disparity; and for 479 finely defined classifications, 35 percent of the disparity was explained.[20] The studies of specific occupations, which tend to explain more of the disparity than more general studies, also confirm this view. This suggests that if the data were available (it generally is not) and one examined very detailed occupations, occupational segregation could explain nearly all of the male-female wage disparity.[21]

These analyses of occupational segregation, however, also fail to resolve the issue of whether the male-female wage disparities are caused by discrimination. First, the human capital studies that include occupation as an explanatory variable generally fail to fully account for the disparity. Any residual may be attributable to discrimination. Second, the limitations of human capital studies that were discussed in connection with the studies of worker characteristics are equally present in these studies. Third, and most significantly, if these studies did fully explain the disparity, it would mean that the disparity is caused by the differing occupations held by male and female workers. But this fails to resolve the discrimination issue since it may be that men and women are employed in different occupations because of discrimination. Thus, the analysis of occupational segregation merely serves to refocus the discrimination issue. The issue changes from whether the male-female wage disparity is caused by sex discrimination to whether occupational segregation is caused by sex discrimination. One commentator has referred to this as an exercise in pillow punching.[22]

There are two main approaches to the issue of whether occupational segregation is caused by sex discrimination. The first is, once again, a human capital approach that is based on neoclassical assumptions of perfect competition. Under this approach, occupational segregation may occur in a non-discriminatory environment. The second approach relies on the structure of labor markets and tends to indicate that discrimination plays a role in occupational segregation.

The human capital approach begins with an economic theory of the family and assumptions about the role of women within it. Instead of treating each individual as a profit-maximizing economic unit, this theory views the family as an economic unit that allocates production both in the market and at home and that allocates family investments in human capital. Thus, the family unit engages in a profit-maximizing division of labor. This division of labor, the theory holds, is generally sex-linked, with women bearing the bulk of the production at home and men the bulk of the production in the market. As a consequence, family investment in human capital tends to favor males, who will spend more time in the market where human capital is valued.[23]

This theory's principal use would seem to be to explain male-female wage disparities. If discrimination is defined as unequal pay for equal productivity, wage disparities need not be evidence of discrimination because men and women are not perfect productivity substitutes for one another. Employers pay different wage rates to men and women to compensate for their differing productivities. But the theory has also been used to provide a nondiscriminatory explanation for occupational segregation. According to the theory, women may choose to enter certain types of occupations for a number of reasons related to actual or expected family obligations. Women who expect to leave the workforce to raise children, for example, may choose occupations that are easy to leave and reenter and that do not emphasize lengthy general or firm-specific training. Or women may choose occupations that accommodate family demands—occupations with flexible hours, limited overtime requirements, no travel responsibilities, and so forth. Or, if women expect their labor force participation to be interrupted, they may choose occupations that pay a relatively high initial wage, but that fail to reward work experience with significant wage increases.[24] Women, then, because of their occupational choices and priorities would tend to be limited to a few types of occupations. These occupations would tend to be overcrowded, which would depress wages and discourage men, who do not share the family obligations of women, from entering the occupations. As a result, the human capital approach attributes occupational segregation to the occupational choices made by women and not to discriminatory practices by employers.

The human capital approach in its current state of development, however, is ultimately unsatisfying. Under the approach, one would expect occupations that require lengthy general or firm-specific training to be male-dominated and occupations with easy entry and poor returns for experience to be female-dominated. But occupational segregation cannot be dissected so neatly. There are both male- and female-dominated jobs that require lengthy general training (physicians and nurses, for example); that require lengthy firm-specific training (corporate managers and executive secretaries); and that offer easy entry and poor returns for experience (janitors and waitresses). The human capital approach does not explain why occupations that one would expect to be dominated by one sex are in fact dominated by the other. Moreover, even if accepted, the human capital approach may be more another exercise in pillow punching than a nondiscriminatory explanation of occupational segregation. If occupational segregation is the result of the occupational choices of women, the issue becomes whether those choices were affected by sex discrimination. The human capital approach is not a nondiscriminatory explanation if, as some contend, the range of choices of women is severely restricted by discrimination.[25]

The second approach to the issue of whether occupational segregation is caused by sex discrimination relies on the structure of labor markets and, in particular, on the internal labor markets of large-scale employers. Under this approach, there are two distinct labor markets. Employees new to the firm are hired to port-of-entry positions from an external labor market that closely resembles the neoclassical model. Once an employee enters the firm, however, he or she becomes a part of an internal labor market that fills most of the firm's openings and that operates in accordance with established rules and procedures, such as seniority and job ladders, rather than through direct competition with potential employees in the external labor market. As a result, most positions within a firm are relatively insulated from the competitive forces of the external labor market. The wage rates, and other conditions of employment, are established instead by employers, in some cases in conjunction with employees and unions.[26]

The internal labor market model may contribute to an understanding of occupational segregation. First, the model may explain a type of sex discrimination in hiring. If a vacancy occurs anywhere in the firm and if total employment is to remain unchanged, the firm must hire someone from outside the firm. However, the person hired may work at a job quite remote from the job in which the vacancy occurred. A vacancy in a skilled position, for example, may lead to the hiring of an unskilled laborer, but several persons inside the firm may have been promoted in between. The employer, then, is hiring more for potential productivity (for example, for trainability and longevity) than for current productivity. If employers perceive women as a group to be less likely to be long-term employees and if it is difficult or expensive to determine probable longevity on an individual basis, employers may refuse to hire women.[27] This type of discrimination is called statistical discrimination; because of statistics (or employer perceptions) relating to women as a group, employers may discriminate against all women.

The model also undermines a crucial assumption of human capital theory. Under human capital theory, workers acquire human capital and then seek the jobs that will provide the highest possible return on that investment. But under the internal labor market model, wages and promotional opportunities depend as much on the port-of-entry job one acquires as it does on one's accumulation of human capital. Moreover, the locus of occupational decision making shifts. Under the human capital model, each worker, acting with full information to maximize his returns, makes an occupational choice. Under the internal labor market model, individual workers do not have full information about the complex relationships among a large firm's many job categories. As a result, the employer becomes the primary decision maker by making an assignment to a particular port-of-entry. Occupational segregation, then, may result from employer decisions to place men and women in different port-of-entry jobs. Once again, occupational segregation tends to result more from employer choices (that is, from discrimination) than from the voluntary choices of women relating to human capital investment and returns.

The internal labor market model also helps to explain the persistence of occupational segregation. Under the neoclassical human capital model, discriminatory firms should be restrained by the competitive disadvantages that result from discrimination. Under the internal labor market model, however, most jobs are insulated to some extent from direct market competition. Since workers acquire firm-specific skills, the employer is dependent upon them to fill internal vacancies as they occur, but at the same time workers have very limited mobility. In addition, wage rates cannot be compared to the wage rates of similar jobs in the external labor market because there may not be similar jobs in the external market. Consequently, the range of potential wage rates is quite broad and the actual wage rates depend to a great extent on institutional factors such as the strength of the industry or of the union and the quality of management. Occupational segregation may persist, then, because competitive disadvantages resulting from discrimination may be difficult to identify and evaluate and, indeed, may be completely counterbalanced by institutional factors.

Some economists have expanded the notion of an internal labor market to the labor market as a whole. These economists postulate a dual labor market model, in which there are primary and secondary jobs. The primary sector covers the employers discussed above who develop an internal labor market. Jobs in this sector are characterized by well-defined promotion ladders, stable employment, and relatively good wages and working conditions. The secondary sector covers jobs that are not as insulated from competitive market pressures. The jobs are likely to be in industries with low capital investment, low unionization and low profit margins, and the jobs themselves are likely to be low-paying, with high turnover and little chance for promotion. Jobs in the primary sector, perhaps because of statistical discrimination or because of the degree of insulation from market pressures, tend to be dominated by men, while jobs in the secondary sector tend to be dominated by women.

The dual labor market model is a logical outgrowth of the internal labor market model. Employers emphasizing potential productivity, and in particular longevity, do not hire women for jobs in the primary sector. Women are thus relegated to the secondary sector, where they receive a low yield on the human capital investment that they have made. Women, then, have little incentive to make further human capital investments, which reinforces employer decisions to exclude them from the primary sector. This type of feedback mechanism aggravates the segregative effect of internal labor markets.

Although the dual labor market model provides some insights, it is not, ultimately, a satisfying explanation of occupational segregation. The labor market as a whole cannot be divided neatly into primary and secondary sectors. Jobs instead fall on a continuum with no clear dividing line between those in the primary and those in the secondary sector. Moreover, the model does not explain why some jobs in the secondary sector are female-dominated while others are male-dominated, nor does the model explain differential treatment accorded to men and women within the primary sector.

In summary, the studies that have focused on occupational segregation as the explanation for the male-female wage disparity also fail to resolve the discrimination issue. Although the disparity is better explained by occupation and worker characteristics than it is by worker characteristics alone, the studies cannot account for the total disparity and any residual may be attributable to discrimination. Even if the studies could account for the total disparity, sex discrimination could not be ruled out as a causative factor because it may be that occupational segregation itself is caused by discrimination.

The Economic Consequences of Comparable Worth

Economic analysis also enables us to assess the probable economic consequences if comparable worth is implemented. This type of analysis is necessary to evaluate the claims of advocacy groups on this issue. Employer organizations have estimated that the cost of implementation would be $320 billion and that there would be dire economic consequences.[28] Groups that favor comparable worth, of course, have a much different perspective. This section assesses the economic ramifications of implementing and of not implementing comparable worth.

It is not easy to assess even the direct cost of implementing comparable worth, but there is no doubt that it would be costly. Comparable worth theory requires that the compensation rates for jobs occupied predominately by women be increased to the extent they are depreciated by sex discrimination. Treiman, Hartmann, and Roos have provided one calculation of the pay adjustments that would be required to do that.[29] Based on 1970 census data, it would be necessary to increase the annual earnings of persons employed in female-dominated occupations $2,383, from $4,564 to $6,947, to remove the net effect of sex composition on the pay rates of female-dominated occupations. In 1980, there were 10.5 million persons employed in these occupations, so the direct cost of implementing comparable worth theory would be about $25 billion.

This estimate, of course, is very crude. It overestimates the cost of implementing comparable worth because it assumes that all persons employed in female-dominated occupations would have their pay rates adjusted. In reality, many persons working in female-dominated occupations are employed by employers who are not covered by the employment discrimination laws[30] and others are employed by employers that, although sufficiently large to be covered by the employment discrimination laws, are so small that the costs of bringing a lawsuit to enforce any legal right to a pay adjustment would outweigh the benefits that might be obtained.[31] As a result, many persons included in the cost estimate above would probably never receive a pay adjustment. The direct cost figure underestimates the cost of implementing comparable worth because it includes as female-dominated occupations only those occupations that have 70 percent or more female incumbents. Theoretically, pay rates should be increased for all occupations, not just female-dominated occupation, that have had their pay rates depreciated because of the sex of their incumbents. Treiman, Hartmann and Roos have estimated that to eliminate the effect of sex composition in occupations that have between 10 and 70 percent female incumbents, it would be necessary to increase the annual earnings of persons in those occupations $850.[32] If comparable worth were implemented this thoroughly, the costs would be greatly increased.

Opponents of comparable worth contend that direct costs are only one aspect of the economic consequences of implementation. Inflation and unemployment are indirect costs of implementation that must also be considered.[33] Implementation would require employers to increase the wages of persons in female-dominated jobs, but productivity would remain constant. As a result, other groups must receive less. Employers may raise prices to recoup their increased costs. If they do, inflation would result and groups that cannot protect themselves from inflation, such as retired and disabled persons, will receive less. Some have predicted that nationwide implementation of comparable worth would increase the inflation rate by 9.7 percent[34] Alternatively, employers might reduce the number of persons that they employ in female-dominated occupations. They might substitute capital for labor; for example, they might buy computers for word processing so that they do not need to employ as many secretaries. Or they might simply devote more of their resources to types of production that do not require the employment of as many persons in female-dominated occupations. Either reaction is likely to increase unemployment and increase it disproportionately in female-dominated occupations.

Proponents of comparable worth argue that the direct and indirect costs of implementation are relevant but must be viewed in context. As a matter of theory, the direct costs of comparable worth are required to eliminate the direct effect of discrimination on the salaries of female-dominated occupations. To proponents, the issue is whether these costs of discrimination should be borne in the first instance by employers or by persons in female-dominated occupations. Implementation would impose the costs on employers; failure to implement would impose the costs on persons in female-dominated occupations. Proponents give moral and practical reasons for imposing these costs on employers. Morally, employers bear some responsibility for the discrimination in market rates, while workers in female-dominated occupations are victims of discrimination. Practically, employers are more able to shift these costs and, hence, distribute the costs throughout society. Employers, for example, may attempt to recoup costs by raising prices, which would tend to shift the costs to consumers, who may have benefited from the discrimination in the past. Persons employed in female-dominated occupations do not have the ability to shift costs and, hence, would have to bear the entire burden of this type of discrimination themselves. While steps should be taken to minimize the costs of implementation, the costs do not justify imposing the continuing costs of this type of discrimination on innocent victims, that is, on persons employed in female-dominated occupations.

In summary, economics cannot provide any firm answers on this issue either. A full implementation of comparable worth would clearly be quite costly and would probably affect the rates of unemployment and inflation. Proponents argue, however, that a failure to implement would also be costly and would impose all of the costs on the victims of discrimination.

Comments and Perspective

Comparable worth theory requires adjustments in wage rates if males and females are compensated differently because of sex discrimination. There is, without question, a significant disparity between the earnings of women as a group and the earnings of men as a group. The difficult question is whether this disparity is caused in whole or in part by sex discrimination.

The mere existence of an earnings disparity is not sufficient evidence of discrimination to warrant wage adjustments. Differences in earnings are the result of a number of complex forces, only some of which are discriminatory. Some commentators contend that if all discrimination were removed from the labor market overnight, the disparity would narrow, but women would still be likely to earn only about 80 percent of what men earn.[35] Two types of economic analysis, however, suggest that the disparity is caused in substantial part by discrimination. Human capital studies of worker characteristics can explain only a portion of the male-female wage disparity and the inference is that the unexplained portion is attributable to discrimination. Similar studies of worker characteristics and occupation also explain only a portion, albeit a larger portion, of the wage disparity and, once again, the inference is that the unexplained portion is attributable to discrimination.

These studies and economic analysis in general, however, cannot definitively answer the causation question. Economists cannot agree on an underlying theoretical basis for their research and, even if they could, practical implementation problems would preclude a definitive answer.

The issue, then, must change from an economic question to a legal and political question: How certain must one be that male-female wage disparities are caused by discrimination before action is taken to rectify the disparity? That issue has been addressed by the courts and by political bodies and will be discussed in more detail in later chapters of this book. A relevant issue in the political debate, however, involves the economic consequences of implementing comparable worth. Economics, although helpful, cannot definitely pinpoint the costs. Although implementation would clearly be costly, economics cannot weigh those costs against the equally undesirable costs arising from failure to implement comparable worth.

2
Comparable Worth Litigation

The courts have been a major forum for comparable worth debate. The issue exploded into the national consciousness when a lower federal court in Washington found the state liable for millions of dollars in damages using comparable worth theory.[1] Other courts have split; some seem to accept comparable worth as a viable legal theory,[2] while others reject it with unequivocal language.[3] Dozens of cases are currently pending in the federal courts.

The courts have played this central role in the development of comparable worth theory for several reasons. First, comparable worth, properly defined, is a sex discrimination issue and the laws that outlaw such discrimination repose a great deal of discretion in the courts. Second, unlike legislatures, which can table or refuse to consider bills addressing the issue, the courts must address comparable worth claims if they are presented. Third, comparable worth claims are prototypical examples of the kinds of cases that are unlikely to be settled and, hence, are likely to be litigated: the law is in a very uncertain state, the potential damages are very large, the parties often have dramatically conflicting ideologies, and the cases are heavily publicized. Finally, the courts are particularly well-suited forums for this type of case. Courts in our society are used not only to resolve disputes between individual litigants, but also, especially in cases involving civil rights, to articulate and to mold social attitudes and values.

The Legal Setting

The issue of comparable worth first arose in Congress in 1961 and 1962 as Congress considered bills that eventually resulted in the Equal Pay Act of 1963.[4] These early bills required equal pay for men and women "for work of comparable character on jobs the performance of which requires comparable skills."[5] Comparable meant then what it means today. The bills would have required employers to pay male- and female-dominated jobs equally if they were rated equivalent under a job evaluation system.

But these bills were not enacted into law as originally written. Representative St. George moved to substitute the word equal for the word comparable, and that change made its way into the bill that was eventually enacted into law.[6] The Equal Pay Act of 1963 required equal pay for men and women only for "equal work" on jobs that require "equal skill, effort, and responsibility and which are performed under similar working conditions."[7] Representative Goodell later explained the change:

> [W]hen the House changed the word "comparable" to "equal" the clear intention was to narrow the whole concept. We went from "comparable" to "equal" meaning that the jobs should be virtually identical, that is they would be very much alike or closely related to each other.[8]

The Equal Pay Act, then, is not a tool that can be used to address the comparable worth issue. The Equal Pay Act is violated only if men and women are performing the same, or virtually identical, work and one sex is paid less than the other. Thus, if Freeda Peeples, a female nurse, is paid less than male nurses, the Equal Pay Act provides a remedy.[9] The Equal Pay Act simply does not apply if men and women are performing different work. So if Freeda Peeples is paid less than male janitors, the Equal Pay Act is not violated even if Freeda can prove that nursing requires greater skill, effort, and responsibility and is performed under less-favorable working conditions.

In 1964, Congress was again considering an antidiscrimination bill. This bill would have made it illegal for an employer to discriminate on the basis of race, color, religion, or national origin.[10] Representative Smith, hoping to create a bill that could be defeated, proposed that the bill also prohibit sex discrimination.[11] The prohibition on sex discrimination was added, but the strategy to defeat the bill failed. Title VII of the Civil Rights Act of 1964, then, contained a broad prohibition on sex discrimination in employment.[12]

Congress, however, was not clear on whether Title VII should apply to comparable worth claims. Congress had, after all, just rejected a comparable worth standard when it enacted the Equal Pay Act in 1963. Title VII contained a provision, commonly called the Bennett Amendment, which was intended to resolve conflicts between Title VII and the Equal Pay Act, but the provision was ambiguous. In the case set out below, the United States Supreme Court considered whether Title VII applied to a sex-based wage compensation claim, similar to comparable worth claims.

County of Washington v. Gunther
452 U.S. 161 (1981)

JUSTICE BRENNAN delivered the opinion of the Court.

The question presented is whether [Section] 703(h) of Title VII of the Civil Rights Act of 1964 restricts Title VII's prohibition of sex-based wage discrimination to claims of equal pay for equal work.

I

This case arises over the payment by petitioner County of Washington, Ore., of substantially lower wages to female guards in the female section of the county jail than it paid to male guards in the male section of the jail. Respondents are four women who were employed to guard female prisoners and to carry out certain other functions in the jail. . . . They alleged that they were paid unequal wages for work substantially equal to that performed by male guards, and in the alternative, that part of the pay differential was attributable to intentional sex discrimination. The latter allegation was based on a claim that, because of intentional discrimination, the county set the pay scale for female guards, but not for male guards, at a level lower than that warranted by its own survey of outside markets and the worth of the jobs.

After trial, the District Court found that the male guards supervised more than 10 times as many prisoners per guard as did the female guards, and that the females devoted much of their time to less valuable clerical duties. It therefore held that respondents' jobs were not substantially equal to those of the male guards, and that respondents were thus not entitled to equal pay. The Court of Appeals affirmed on that issue, and respondents do not seek review of the ruling.

The District Court also dismissed respondents' claim that the discrepancy in pay between the male and female guards was attributable in part to intentional sex discrimination. It held as a matter of law that a sex-based wage discrimination claim cannot be brought under Title VII unless it would satisfy the equal work standard of the Equal Pay Act of 1963. The court therefore permitted no additional evidence on this claim, and made no findings on whether petitioner county's pay scales for female guards resulted from intentional sex discrimination.

We emphasize at the outset the narrowness of the question before us in this case. Respondents' claim is not based on the controversial concept of "comparable worth," under which plaintiffs might claim increased compensation on the basis of a comparison of the intrinsic worth or difficulty of their job with that of other jobs in the same organization or community. Rather, respondents seek to prove, by direct evidence, that their wages were depressed because of intentional sex discrimination, consisting of setting the wage scale for female guards, but not for male guards, at a level lower than its own survey of outside markets and the worth of the jobs warranted. The narrow question in this case is whether such a claim is precluded by the last sentence of [Section] 703(h) of Title VII, called the "Bennett Amendment."

II

Title VII makes it an unlawful employment practice for an employer "to discriminate against any individual with respect to his compensation, terms, conditions, or privileges of employment, because of such individual's ... sex. . . ." The Bennett Amendment to Title VII, however, provides:

> It shall not be an unlawful employment practice under this subchapter for any employer to differentiate upon the basis of sex in determining the amount of wages or compensation paid or to be paid to employees of such employer if such differentiation is authorized by the [Equal Pay Act].

To discover what practices are exempted from Title VII's prohibitions by the Bennett Amendment, we must turn to the Equal Pay Act. On its face, the Equal Pay Act contains three restrictions pertinent to this case. First, its coverage is limited to those employers subject to the Fair Labor Standards Act. Thus, the Act does not apply, for example, to certain businesses engaged in retail sales, fishing, agriculture, and newspaper publishing. Second, the Act is restricted to cases involving "equal work on jobs the performance of which requires equal skill, effort, and responsibility, and which are performed under similar working conditions." Third, the Act's four affirmative defenses exempt any wage differentials attributable to seniority, merit, quantity or quality of production, or "any other factor other than sex."

Petitioners argue that the purpose of the Bennett Amendment was to restrict Title VII sex-based wage discrimination claims to those that could also be brought under the Equal Pay Act, and thus that claims not arising from "equal work" are precluded. Respondents, in contrast, argue that the Bennett Amendment was designed merely to incorporate the four affirmative defenses of the Equal Pay Act into Title VII for sex-based wage discrimination claims. Respondents thus contend that claims for sex-based wage discrimination can be brought under Title VII even though no member of the opposite sex holds an equal but higher paying job, provided that the challenged wage rate is not based on seniority, merit, quantity or quality of production, or "any other factor other than sex." While recognizing that the language and legislative history of the provision are not unambiguous, we conclude that the [respondents are] correct.

A

The language of the Bennett Amendment suggests an intention to incorporate only the affirmative defenses of the Equal Pay Act into Title VII. The Amendment bars sex-based wage discrimination claims under Title VII where the pay differential is "authorized" by the Equal Pay Act. Although the word "authorize" sometimes means simply "to permit," it ordinarily denotes affirmative enabling action. Black's Law Dictionary 122 (5th ed. 1979) defines "authorize" as "[t]o empower; to give a right or authority to act." The question, then, is what wage practices have been affirmatively authorized by the Equal Pay Act.

The Equal Pay Act is divided into two parts: a definition of the violation, followed by four affirmative defenses. The first part can hardly be said to "authorize" anything at all: it is purely prohibitory. The second part, however, in essence "authorizes" employers to differentiate in pay on the basis of seniority, merit, quantity or quality of production, or any other factor other than sex, even though such differentiation might otherwise violate the Act. It is to these provisions, therefore, that the Bennett Amendement must refer.

Petitioners argue that this construction of the Bennett Amendment would render it superfluous. Petitioners claim that the first three affirmative defenses are simply redundant of the provisions elsewhere in [Section] 703(h) of Title VII that already exempt bona fide seniority and merit systems and systems measuring earnings by quantity or quality of production, and that the fourth defense—"any other factor other than sex"—is implicit in Title VII's general prohibition of sex-based discrimination.

We cannot agree. The Bennett Amendment was offered as a "technical amendment" designed to resolve any potential conflicts between Title VII and the Equal Pay Act. Thus, with respect to the first three defenses, the Bennett Amendment has the effect of guaranteeing that courts and administrative agencies adopt a consistent interpretation of like provisions in both statutes. Otherwise, they might develop inconsistent bodies of case law interpreting two sets of nearly identical language.

More importantly, incorporation of the fourth affirmative defense could have significant consequences for Title VII litigation. Title VII's prohibition of discriminatory employment practices was intended to be broadly inclusive, proscribing "not only overt discrimination but also practices that are fair in form, but discriminatory in operation." The structure of Title VII litigation, including presumptions, burdens of proof, and defenses, has been designed to reflect this approach. The fourth affirmative defense of the Equal Pay Act, however, was designed differently, to confine the application of the Act to wage differentials attributable to sex discrimination. Equal Pay Act litigation, therefore, has been structured to permit employers to defend against charges of discrimination where their pay differentials are based on bona fide use of "other factors other than sex." Although we do not decide in this case how sex-based wage discrimination litigation under Title VII should be structured to accomodate the fourth affirmative defense of the Equal Pay Act, we consider it clear that the Bennett Amendment, under this interpretation, is not rendered superfluous.

We therefore conclude that only differentials attributable to the four affirmative defenses of the Equal Pay Act are "authorized" by that Act within the meaning of [Section] 703(h) of Title VII.

B

The legislative background of the Bennett Amendment is fully consistent with this interpretation.

Title VII was the second bill relating to employment discrimination to be enacted by the 88th Congress. Earlier, the same Congress passed the Equal Pay Act. Any possible inconsistency between the Equal Pay Act and Title VII did not surface until late in the debate over Title VII in the House of Representatives, because, until then, Title VII extended only to discrimination based on race, color, religion, or national origin, while the Equal Pay Act applied only to sex discrimination. Just two days before voting on Title VII, the House of Representatives amended the bill to proscribe sex discrimination, but did not discuss the implications of the overlapping jurisdiction of Title VII, as amended, and the Equal Pay Act. The Senate took up consideration of the House version of the Civil Rights bill without reference to any committee. Thus, neither House of Congress had the opportunity to undertake formal analysis of the relation between the two statutes.

Several Senators expressed concern that insufficient attention had been paid to possible inconsistencies between the statutes. In an attempt to rectify the problem, Senator Bennett proposed his amendment. The Senate leadership approved the proposal as a "technical amendment" to the Civil Rights bill, and it was taken up on the floor on June 12, 1964, after cloture had been invoked. The Amendment engendered no controversy, and passed without recorded vote. The entire discussion comprised a few short statements [by Senators Bennett and Dirksen].

The discussion shows that Senator Bennett proposed the Amendment because of a general concern that insufficient attention had been paid to the relation between the Equal Pay Act and Title VII, rather than because of a *specific* potential conflict between the statutes. His explanation that the Amendment assured that the provisions of the Equal Pay Act "shall not be nullified" in the event of conflict with Title VII may be read as referring to the affirmative defenses of the Act. Indeed, his emphasis on the "technical" nature of the Amendment and his concern for not disrupting the "effective administration" of the Equal Pay Act are more compatible with an interpretation of the Amendment as incorporating the Act's affirmative defenses, as administratively interpreted, than as engrafting all the restrictive features of the Equal Pay Act onto Title VII.

Senator Dirksen's comment that all that the Bennett Amendment does is to "recognize" the exceptions carried in the Fair Labor Standards Act, suggests that the Bennett Amendment was necessary because of the exceptions to coverage in the Fair Labor Standards Act, which made the Equal Pay Act applicable to a narrower class of employers than was Title VII. The Bennett Amendment clarified that the standards of the Equal Pay Act would govern even those wage discrimination cases where only Title VII would otherwise apply. So understood, Senator Dirksen's remarks are not inconsistent with our interpretation.

Although there was no debate on the Bennett Amendment in the House of Representatives when the Senate version of the Act returned for final approval, Representative Celler explained each of the Senate's amendments immediately prior to the vote. He stated that the Bennett Amendment "[p]rovides that compliance with the Fair Labor Standards Act as amended satisfies the requirement of the title barring discrimination because of sex. . . ." If taken literally, this explanation would restrict Title VII's coverage of sex discrimination more severely than even petitioners suggest: not only would it confine *wage discrimination* claims to those actionable under the Equal Pay Act, but it would block *all other* sex discrimination claims as well. We can only conclude that Representative Celler's explanation was not intended to be precise, and does not provide a solution to the present problem.

Thus, although the few references by Members of Congress to the Bennett Amendment do not explicitly confirm that its purpose was to incorporate into Title VII the four affirmative defenses of the Equal Pay Act in sex-based wage discrimination cases, they are broadly consistent with such a reading, and do not support an alternative reading.

C

The interpretations of the Bennett Amendment by the agency entrusted with administration of Title VII—the Equal Employment Opportunity Commission—do not provide much guidance in this case.

D

Our interpretation of the Bennett Amendment draws additional support from the remedial purposes of Title VII and the Equal Pay Act. Section 703(a) of Title VII makes it unlawful for an employer "to fail or refuse to hire or to discharge any individual, or *otherwise to discriminate* against any individual with respect to his compensation, terms, conditions, or privileges of employment" because of such individual's sex. As Congress itself has indicated, a "broad approach" to the definition of equal employment opportunity is essential to overcoming and undoing the effect of discrimination. We must therefore avoid interpretations of Title VII that deprive victims of discrimination of a remedy, without clear congressional mandate.

Under petitioners' reading of the Bennett Amendment, only those sex-based wage discrimination claims that satisfy the "equal work" standard of the Equal Pay Act could be brought under Title VII. In practical terms, this means that a woman who is discriminatorily underpaid could obtain no relief—no matter how egregious the discrimination might be—unless her employer also employed a man in an equal job in the same establishment, at a higher rate of pay. Thus, if an employer hired a woman for a unique position in the company and then admitted that her salary would have been higher had she been male, the woman would be unable to obtain legal redress under petitioners' interpretation. Similarly, if an employer used a transparently sex-based system for wage determination, women holding jobs not equal to those held by men would be denied the right to prove that the system is a pretext for discrimination. Moreover, to cite an example arising from a recent case *Los Angeles Dept. of Water & Power v. Manhart*, 435 U.S. 702 (1978), if the employer required its female workers to pay more into its pension program than male workers were required to pay, the only women who could bring a Title VII action under petitioners' interpretation would be those who could establish that a man performed equal work: a female auditor thus might have a cause of action while a female secretary might not. Congress surely did not intend the Bennett Amendment to insulate such blatantly discriminatory practices from judicial redress under Title VII.

Moreover, petitioners' interpretation would have other far-reaching consequences. Since it rests on the proposition that any wage differentials not prohibited by the Equal Pay Act are "authorized" by it, petitioners' interpretation would lead to the conclusion that discriminatory compensation by employers not covered by the Fair Labor Standards Act is "authorized"—since not prohibited—by the Equal Pay Act. Thus it would deny Title VII protection against sex-based wage discrimination by those employers not subject to the Fair Labor Standards Act but covered by Title VII. There is no persuasive evidence that Congress intended such a result.

Petitioners' reading is thus flatly inconsistent with our past interpretations of Title VII as "prohibit[ing] all practices in whatever form which create inequality in employment opportunity due to discrimination on the basis of race, religion, sex, or national origin." We must therefore reject petitioners' interpretation of the Bennett Amendment.

III

Petitioners argue strenuously that the approach of the Court of Appeals places "the pay structure of virtually every employer and the entire company . . . at risk and subject to scrutiny by the federal courts." They raise the specter that "Title VII plaintiffs could draw any type of comparison imaginable concerning job duties and pay between any job predominantly performed by women and any job predominantly performed by men." But whatever the merit of petitioners' arguments in other contexts, they are inapplicable here, for claims based on the type of job comparisons petitioners describe are manifestly different from respondents' claim. Respondents contend that the County of Washington evaluated the worth of their jobs; that the county determined that they should be paid approximately 95% as much as the male correctional officers; that it paid them only about 70% as much, while paying the male officers the full evaluated worth of their jobs; and that the failure of the county to pay respondents the full evaluated worth of their jobs can be proved to be attributable to intentional sex discrimination. Thus, respondents' suit does not require a court to make its own subjective assessment of the value of the male and female guard jobs, or to attempt by statistical technique or other method to quantify the effect of sex discrimination on the wage rates.

We do not decide in this case the precise contours of lawsuits challenging sex discrimination in compensation under Title VII. It is sufficient to note that respondents' claims of discriminatory undercompensation are not barred by [Section] 703(h) of Title VII merely because respondents do not perform work equal to that of male jail guards. The judgment of the Court of Appeals is therefore

Affirmed.

The *Gunther* case was critically important for proponents of comparable worth. If the Bennett Amendment had been interpreted to exclude comparable worth claims from Title VII coverage, federal court litigation would not have been available as a mechanism to address the comparable worth issue. For example, even if we were to assume that Freeda Peeples could indisputably prove that the wage differences between nurses and janitors were attributable solely to sex discrimination, litigation would have been futile because no federal law would have prohibited that discrimination. As it is, *Gunther* permits federal court litigation on the comparable worth issue, but it provides little guidance on the shape of that litigation. What must Freeda prove to prevail on her claim that wage differences between nurses and janitors violate Title VII?

Employment Discrimination Theories and Comparable Worth

Title VII prohibits discrimination with very general language: "It shall be [illegal] for an employer . . . to discriminate . . . because of [an] individual's race, color, religion, sex, or national origin."[13] But what is discrimination? The courts have provided two definitions. Under one definition, discrimination occurs when an employer acts with a discriminatory intention or purpose. Thus, if an employer treats Freeda differently because she is a woman, the employer has discriminated. This type of discrimination is called disparate treatment discrimination. The courts have also defined discrimination so as to prohibit employment criteria that have an adverse effect on women and are not required by business considerations, even though the employer does not intend to discriminate. Thus, if an employer requires all employees to weigh at least 180 pounds, the employer has discriminated if weight is not required to adequately perform the job duties. The weight requirement would have an adverse effect on women because it would exclude a much higher proportion of women than men. This type of discrimination is called disparate impact discrimination.

In a comparable worth lawsuit, a plaintiff may rely on both or either type of discrimination.

Disparate Treatment Discrimination

Freeda applies for a job with a hospital. E.M. Ployer, the personnel director for the hospital, decides to hire John, another applicant, rather than Freeda. Did E.M. Ployer discriminate?

Disparate treatment discrimination depends on the state of mind of the employer. If E.M. Ployer did not hire Freeda because she is a woman, he has engaged in illegal discrimination. But if E.M. Ployer failed to hire Freeda for any other reason, he has not discriminated. If E.M. did not hire Freeda because she has less experience than John, or because she went to a less prestigious nursing school than John, or even because Freeda is a blonde and E.M. hires only dark-haired people, E.M. has not discriminated. This last reason may not make sense economically (there is no reason to believe that dark-haired people are more productive employees than blondes), but employers are not required by the law to act economically. They are required only to refrain from making decisions because of a person's sex.

So Freeda, to prove discrimination, must prove that E.M. failed to hire her because she is a woman. But how can Freeda prove that? She could ask E.M. why he hired John rather than her. But E.M. is unlikely to admit that he made the decision because of Freeda's sex, even if he did. The law, then, permits Freeda to prove discrimination with less direct evidence of the employer's state of mind. The following case discusses what evidence Freeda must present to prove discrimination in her simple case. It then goes on to discuss disparate treatment discrimination in a more complex comparable worth case.

Briggs v. City of Madison
536 F. Supp. 435 (W.D. Wis. 1982)

CRABB, Chief Judge.

This is a civil action for declaratory, injunctive and monetary relief, brought against defendant City of Madison pursuant to Title VII of the Civil Rights Act of 1964. Plaintiffs are women employed as public health nurses by the City of Madison Department of Public Health. They allege that defendant discriminates against them on the basis of sex with respect to job compensation, job classification, and the terms, conditions and privileges of their employment by employing them as public health nurses at a lower paying classification than that of male public health sanitarians who perform jobs requiring the same or a lesser degree of qualifications, skill, effort, and responsibility under similar working conditions.

FACTS

Plaintiffs hold positions as public health nurses that have been held exclusively by women since 1958, with one brief exception. From 1958 up through the time of trial, public health nurses have received salaries lower than those paid to the sanitarians who work in the same department for the same employer as do the nurses. From 1958 to 1979, all of the sanitarians have been male.

In terms of pre-hiring requirements, the position of public health nurse has slightly more stringent requirements than the position of sanitarian. Both jobs require a college degree; however, public health nurses must have had specialized training for their positions, whereas sanitarians are recruited from among graduates of a variety of educational programs. Public health nurses must be certified by the State of Wisconsin prior to hiring; sanitarians are not required to have state certification prior to hiring.

In both jobs, the employee must learn a large number of assessment techniques and use a variety of equipment and health assessment aids. In both jobs, the employee is exposed to a wide variety of work assignments.

Public health nurses do some teaching of health in the city's schools. They also do health education for individuals, particularly those who need help in managing a serious or chronic illness or in caring for an infant or handicapped child.

Both sanitarians and public health nurses must exercise tact to persuade persons to initiate corrective action in health-related fields. However, the sanitarian has the backup of license suspension or prosecution by the district or city attorney, whereas the public health nurse has legal backup only with respect to excluding persons with communicable diseases from school or employment. The risk of losing a permit or an operating license provides a strong incentive to comply with a sanitarian's suggestions for corrective action. Except for the sanction of exclusion from work or school, the public health nurse has no comparable authority and must rely more heavily on her own powers of persuasion.

In general, sanitarians deal routinely with persons they know, such as the operators of the bars, restaurants, and motels or managers of apartment houses situated in the sanitarians' area of responsibility. By contrast, much of the public health nurse's work is with persons they [sic] have never seen before, a fair number of whom have difficulty communicating because of language, cultural, mental, or emotional impediments. Public health nurses must exercise diplomacy in their relationships with the principals of the schools to which they are assigned, as it is common for principals to press nurses for diagnoses of particular symptoms, although the nurses are prohibited from making such diagnoses.

Public health nurses meet frequently with other professionals assigned to the city's schools to discuss the needs of particular children whose health problems may affect (or reflect) their emotions, mental ability, and school progress. Frequently, public health nurses will refer a person whom they have seen for health reasons to a city, county, or state agency for assistance and will monitor the referral to insure that contact is made and the necessary assistance is provided.

Both sanitarians and public health nurses have responsibility for the prevention of the kind of errors that could have serious health consequences for individuals or groups of individuals.

Both sanitarians and public health nurses supervise interns. In addition, public health nurses regularly supervise nursing aides in the school who are city employees; sanitarians have no such supervisory responsibility over any other city employee.

Both sanitarians and public health nurses are responsible for the assembling and maintenance of confidential records.

In terms of effort, both sanitarians and public health nurses work regular daytime hours, with little overtime required. Both jobs require the writing of reports and the carrying out of assessment procedures. Both jobs involve driving around the city of Madison, walking and standing on the work site, and some infrequent carrying of equipment and of supplies.

The employees in both jobs are exposed to health hazards, either from exposure to carriers of communicable diseases or from the handling of contaminated food, trash, or offal. They are subject to fairly similar working conditions in that they regularly travel from one work site to another and spend part of each day in performing office duties. However, sanitarians spend more time outside than do the nurses and as a consequence are exposed more frequently to inclement weather.

From the showing made by plaintiffs, a reasonable factfinder could have found that plaintiffs had demonstrated they occupied a sex-segregated job classification that was compensated with lower wages than those paid to the occupants of the all-male classification of sanitarian, that the jobs held by plaintiffs required skill, effort, and responsibility at least equal to, and possibly in excess of, that required of sanitarians by their jobs, and that the jobs were performed under similar working conditions.

OPINION

Plaintiffs contend that they have been discriminated against by the defendant because of their sex; specifically, they assert that they are performing work substantially similar in skill, effort, and responsibility to that performed by the male sanitarians but for which they are paid less.

[I]t seems advisable to emphasize what is not at issue in this case. Plaintiffs are not raising a claim under the Equal Pay Act; they do not contend that public health nurses and sanitarians are performing the same or equal work. Additionally, plaintiffs are not raising a claim of denial of equal access to jobs or promotional opportunities under Title VII. They do not contend that public health nurses are denied the opportunity to compete for sanitarian positions. Rather, plaintiffs' claims rest on a theory that seeks to correlate wage differentials with wage discrimination, where the wage differential applies to sex-segregated jobs of comparable content.

[Let us begin by examining] the purpose and function of a prima facie case in employment discrimination litigation. Essentially, the prima facie case is a means of ordering proof that reflects both a judicial evaluation of the probabilities of the situation and the expectation that the defendant employer has superior access to the proof that will either rebut or support plaintiff's prima facie case.

The use of the prima facie case for employment discrimination lawsuits began in *McDonnell Douglas v. Green,* 411 U.S. 792 (1973), with articulation of a model for ordering and presenting proof in a private discrimination case. The Supreme Court explained that a plaintiff could make the necessary preliminary showing of discrimination by establishing

(i) that he belongs to a racial minority; (ii) that he applied and was qualified for a job for which the employer was seeking applicants; (iii) that, despite his qualifications, he was rejected; and (iv) that, after his rejection, the position remained open and the employer continued to seek applicants from persons of complainant's qualifications.

Id. at 802. The Court noted that the standard for a prima facie case is not inflexible and the prima facie proof may vary depending on the factual situation.

Under the *McDonnell Douglas* formulation, if the plaintiff makes the preliminary showing of discrimination, the "burden then must shift to the employer to articulate some legitimate, nondiscriminatory reason for the employer's rejection." *Id.* If the employer advances such a reason, the plaintiff then has an opportunity to show that the reason stated by the employer is in fact pretextual. The value of this model lies in the fact that it is "a sensible, orderly way to evaluate the evidence in light of common experience as it bears on the critical question of discrimination," *Furnco Construction Co. v. Waters,* 438 U.S. 567, 577 (1978).

> A prima facie case under *McDonnell Douglas* raises an inference of discrimination only because we presume these acts, if otherwise unexplained, are more likely than not based on the consideration of impermissible facts. And we are willing to presume this largely because we know from our experience that more often than not people do not act in a totally arbitrary manner, without any underlying reasons, especially in a business setting. Thus, when all legitimate reasons for rejecting an applicant have been eliminated as possible reasons for the employer's actions, it is more likely than not the employer, who we generally assume acts only with some reason, based his decision on an impermissible consideration such as race.

Id.

I have found that a reasonable factfinder could have found at the close of plaintiffs' case-in-chief that plaintiffs had proved each element of what they contend makes out a prima facie case; that is, they have proved that 1) they are members of a protected class; 2) that they occupy a sex-segregated classification; 3) that they are paid less than 4) a sex-segregated classification occupied by men; and also 5) that the two sex-segregated classifications involve work that is similar in skill, effort, and responsibility.

The critical question is whether a reasonable factfinder could infer from a showing of the first four elements, or from all five, that it is more probable than not that the defendant engaged in an employment practice made unlawful by Title VII.

With respect to plaintiffs' first, four-part formulation, I conclude that the inference cannot be drawn and therefore, that no prima facie case is made out. The four-part formulation does not eliminate the most common, nondiscriminatory reason for wage disparity: differences in the jobs' requirements of skill, effort, and responsibility.

I am aware that there is a body of opinion that holds that there is a demonstrable correlation between sex- (or race-) segregated jobs and lower wages. This opinion is articulated by many, most forcefully by Ruth Blumrosen. Blumrosen has posited the thesis that no more is necessary to a prima facie case of legally impermissible wage discrimination than a showing of past or present job segregation by race or sex. *See* Blumrosen, *Wage Discrimination, Job Segregation and Title VII of the Civil Rights Act of 1964,* 12 U. Mich. J.L. Ref. 397 (1979).

The elements of Blumrosen's theory can be summarized as follows: job segregation and wage discrimination are intimately related; whenever there is job segregation, the same forces that determine that certain jobs will be reserved for women or minorities determine that the economic value of such jobs is low; studies undertaken in the field of history, anthropology, economics, and sociology demonstrate that the valuation of segregated jobs has been influenced by the fact that these jobs are held by disfavored groups; therefore in a lawsuit, minorities or women who can demonstrate that they occupy traditionally segregated jobs will have made a prima facie showing that the wage rates for those jobs are discriminatorily depressed, so that the burden is on the defendant employer to demonstrate or articulate the reasons why the rate is not influenced by discriminatory factors.

I find unpersuasive the basic premise that Blumrosen or any one possesses the intellectual tools and data base that would enable them to identify the extent to which the factor of discrimination has contributed to, or created, sex-segregated jobs, and to separate that factor from the myriad of nondiscriminatory factors that may have contributed to the same result. Equally unpersuasive is the contention that a direct correlation can be shown to exist between the lower pay scales for jobs characterized as "women's work" and the fact that the jobs are so characterized. Although I share the belief that there is probably some correlation, I do not share Blumrosen's conviction that the job characterization factor is the only determinative of pay scales. In making this assertion, Blumrosen ignores other potentially determinative factors, such as "crowding" (a heavy concentration of women available for the same job), the willingness or unwillingness of women to organize for higher wages and increased benefits, and the historical reality that many of the jobs characterized by Blumrosen and others as "women's work" are jobs that have never been well-compensated, whether they have been filled by women or by men.

For purposes of litigation, Blumrosen's thesis suffers also from its exclusive focus upon historical events and societal attitudes, rather than upon allegedly unlawful acts of the employer who is the defendant in the lawsuit. The plain language of Title VII indicates the Congressional intent to influence and affect the conduct of employers. The statute's prohibitions are directed at the employer's employment practices; the statute's sanctions are directed at the employer who violates the prohibitions and engages in an unlawful employment practice. The statute's remedial purpose is not so broad as to make employers liable for employment practices of others or for existing market conditions.

The mere showing that plaintiffs are women occupying a sex-segregated job classification in which they are paid less than men occupying a sex-segregated job classification fails to make a prima facie case. More than this is required to implicate the defendant and to permit the drawing of an inference of impermissible acts of discrimination by the City.

I turn then to plaintiffs' alternative formulation that adds the fifth factor of the similarity of the requirements of the two jobs at issue to the showing that 1) plaintiffs are members of a protected class 2) who occupy a sex-segregated job classification 3) that is paid less than a 4) sex-segregated job classification occupied by men. I conclude that, unlike plaintiffs' first formulation, this model does constitute a prima facie showing. It rests upon the logical premise that jobs which are similar in their requirements of skill, effort, and responsibility and in their working conditions are of comparable value to an employer, and upon the equally logical premise that jobs of comparable value would be compensated comparably but for the employer's discriminatory treatment of the lower-paid employees.

To be explicit, I find that plaintiffs have made a prima facie case of sex discrimination by showing that (1) they are members of a protected class (2) occupying a sex-segregated job classification (3) that is paid less than a (4) sex-segregated job classification occupied by men and (5) that the two job classifications at issue are so similar in their requirements of skill, effort, and responsibility, and working conditions that it can reasonably be inferred that they are of comparable value to an employer.

Although other factors may enter into the compensation determination, it is the factors of skill, effort, responsibility and working conditions that are most commonly determinative of the wage rate. By eliminating these factors in their prima facie case as an explanation for a differential in wage rates plaintiffs have eliminated the most common defense to a pay discrimination case brought pursuant to Title VII.

Because plaintiffs have presented a prima facie case of sex discrimination, it becomes defendant's burden to produce evidence of legitimate, nondiscriminatory reasons for the differential in pay ranges. At trial, defendant adduced evidence of the higher wages paid to sanitarians working for the state, and of comparable salaries paid to municipally-employed sanitarians throughout the state. Health Director Kincaid testified about the difficulties he had experienced in trying to attract qualified sanitarians to work for the City and his efforts to obtain higher salaries for this job to make recruiting easier.

This evidence raises a genuine issue of fact as to whether defendant discriminated illegally against plaintiffs. The evidence offered by Kincaid indicates that the two adjustments in the pay ranges made for the sanitarians were the result of perceived difficulties in the recruitment and retention of persons qualified to perform this particular job.

Plaintiffs contend that it is no defense for defendant to point to market demands (or its perception of market demands) as justification for upgrading the pay ranges of the male sanitarians but not the pay ranges of the public health nurses. They argue, first, that the market reflects the biases and stereotypes of the value of women's work, and, in particular, reflects the devaluation of nurses' salaries resulting from female domination of the nursing field; second, that reliance on the market has been rejected in Equal Pay Act cases and should be rejected here for similar reasons; and third, that defendant's proffered explanation of reliance on the market is suspect in view of the evidence that defendant looked to the market only in setting sanitarian salaries and not in setting nursing salaries.

I find plaintiffs' first argument unpersuasive for the reason discussed earlier in this opinion. Under Title VII, an employer's liability extends only to its own acts of discrimination. Nothing in the Act indicates that the employer's liability extends to conditions of the marketplace which it did not create. Nothing indicates that it is improper for an employer to pay the wage rates necessary to compete in the marketplace for qualified job applicants. That there may be an abundance of applicants qualified for some jobs and a dearth of skilled applicants for other jobs is not a condition for which a particular employer bears responsibility.

Plaintiffs' second argument rests on decisions in Equal Pay Act cases holding that employers can not justify wage disparities between males and females performing equal work by asserting the greater difficulty of recruiting men for those jobs. Those decisions are inapposite in a case such as this where plaintiffs are contending not that essentially *identical* skills are required for both of the jobs at issue, but rather, that the kinds of skills are closely related and that the skills are substantially similar in the amount of education and levels of the on-the-job training required. In the cited Equal Pay Act cases, the jobs were so similar as to be interchangeable; that is, a female worker could perform the job held by male workers, if given the opportunity, and vice versa. Where, however, different skills are required for the performances of the jobs, the employer may explain and justify an apparent illegal wage disparity by showing that persons possessing the requisite skills are commanding higher wage rates in the local market.

Plaintiffs' third argument goes to the credibility of defendant's explanation and will be considered in the discussion of the sufficiency of plaintiffs' rebuttal case.

Once defendant meets its burden, then the plaintiffs have an opportunity to challenge the validity of defendant's explanation as part of plaintiffs' ultimate burden of persuading the court that they have been the victims of discrimination motivated by illegal intent on the part of their employer.

At this third stage of the trial plaintiffs' case fails for lack of proof either that it is more likely than not that a discriminatory reason motivated defendant in creating or retaining the pay disparity between the public health nurses and the sanitarians or, alternatively, that the explanation offered by defendant is unworthy of credence. Specifically, plaintiffs did not show that defendant's upgrading of the sanitarians' pay ranges was not a response to a legitimate perception that pay increases were necessary in order to recruit and retain qualified sanitarians.

In order to show that defendant's explanation of its actions was not credible or that it was only a pretext, plaintiffs [adduced] evidence tending to indicate that nursing vacancies occurred, that these vacancies were not always filled promptly, and that, on several occasions in 1967, the Director of Nursing had expressed concern to director Kincaid about nursing vacancies and nurses' salaries. On the strength of this evidence, plaintiffs argue that defendant's explanation for upgrading sanitarian pay is not credible; that defendant's greater concern about sanitarian salaries and sanitarian vacancies is not a defense to the charge of sex discrimination but a reflection of its greater concern for, and its more favorable treatment of, male employees.

Plaintiffs may be accurate in their perception, but they have failed to produce the kind of hard evidence about the general availability of both sanitarians and public health nurses in the labor market during the time in question that would suffice to carry their burden of persuasion. If they wish to show that director Kincaid had no reasonable basis for his beliefs that higher salaries were necessary to retain and recruit sanitarians and not necessary to retain and recruit qualified public health nurses, they will have to show more than they have shown in this case about the relative availability of qualified nurses and sanitarians, about the occurrence and duration of vacancies in both categories of jobs, or about the relative impact of a vacancy upon the nursing staff and the sanitarian staff.

In summary, I find and conclude . . . that plaintiffs have failed to carry their ultimate burden of persuading this court that they have been the victims of intentional discrimination made illegal under Title VII of the Civil Rights Act.

As *Briggs* indicates, there are three stages to a disparate treatment case. First, the plaintiff must create an inference of discrimination. Then, the employer has an opportunity to rebut by articulating a legitimate, nondiscriminatory reason for the challenged decision. Finally, the plaintiff has the burden of demonstrating that the reason stated by the employer is pretextual.

This model works well in a simple case like Freeda Peeple's. Freeda's initial burden of creating an inference of discrimination is not onerous. She must prove that she applied and was qualified for a job for which the hospital was seeking applicants and that she was rejected. Thus, Freeda might present evidence that she applied for a nursing position with the hospital, that she is a registered nurse, that the hospital was advertising job openings for registered nurses, and that she was not hired. With this proof, Freeda creates an inference of discrimination by eliminating the most common nondiscriminatory reasons—no job opening and lack of qualifications—for her rejection. If the hospital fails to present any evidence to rebut Freeda's case, Freeda prevails because of the inference.

The hospital, however, has an opportunity to rebut Freeda's case. The hospital's burden at this stage, like Freeda's initial burden, is not onerous. The hospital must articulate a legitimate, nondiscriminatory reason for its decision. E.M. Ployer might testify, for example, that Freeda was not hired because she was not sufficiently experienced. If no other evidence is presented, the hospital would prevail because it has rebutted the inference of discrimination created by Freeda; it has supplied a legitimate, nondiscriminatory reason for its decision. Requiring the hospital to explain its decision at this stage, then, serves to frame the factual issue of the case. If the true reason for Freeda's rejection was her lack of experience, the hospital prevails. If Freeda can show that her lack of experience was not the true reason, the inference of discrimination she initially created is revived and she would prevail.

After the hospital's showing, then, Freeda has the burden of proving that the proffered reason (lack of experience) was not the true reason for her rejection. Freeda might do this, for example, by showing that the person hired by the hospital instead of her had less experience than she did, or by showing that the hospital had not considered experience as a factor in making employment decisions in the past.

The weaknesses in this model for proving disparate treatment discrimination are exposed when it is applied in a complex comparable worth case. Plaintiffs' initial burden of creating an inference of discrimination is more onerous in a comparable worth case. Plaintiffs had argued in *Briggs* that an inference of discrimination is created merely by showing that a female-dominated job classification (nurses) is paid less than a male-dominated job classification (sanitarians). Or, to use a more revealing example, an inference of discrimination would arise under this formulation if evidence were presented that secretaries were paid less than brain surgeons. But the Court held that evidence of a wage disparity between two sex-dominated occupations is not sufficient, by itself, to create an inference of discrimination because it does not eliminate the most common nondiscriminatory reason for a wage disparity: differences in the skill, effort, and responsibility required by the jobs. Thus, to create an inference, plaintiffs must also prove that the two sex-segregated job classifications involve work that is comparable in skill, effort, and responsibility.

The comparable work requirement, however, presents it own problems. First, there is the problem of how to prove that different jobs require comparable skill, effort, and responsibility. In *Briggs,* the jobs being compared were quite similar and the Court relied on a nonexpert evaluation of the requirements of the two jobs to establish this element of the plaintiffs' case. In most cases, though, the jobs will not be so similar. In one case, plaintiffs compared food service workers with truck drivers and nurse practitioners with boiler operators. To compare such dissimilar jobs, a formal job evaluation must be conducted. Formal job evaluations will be discussed in more detail in chapter 3, but suffice it to say here that they are expensive and involve significant elements of uncertainty and subjectivity. The expense is troublesome because it means that small employers may be immune from comparable worth lawsuits and, hence, that some discrimination of this type may go unredressed. The uncertainty and subjectivity is troublesome because it tends to undermine the reliability of a finding of discrimination based in part on a job evaluation.

Even if job evaluations could be done reliably and inexpensively, is the showing required of plaintiffs to establish a prima facie case sufficient to create an inference of discrimination? Certainly, there may be other common and nondiscriminatory reasons for the wage disparity. The sanitarians, for example, may be unionized while the nurses are not, or there may be supply and demand differences between the two jobs. Should plaintiffs be required to eliminate these explanations for a wage disparity to create an inference of discrimination? *Briggs* answers that question no and thus requires the employer to forward other nondiscriminatory explanations for the wage disparity.

The employer's burden in a comparable worth case mirrors quite closely the employer's burden in a simple case. In a simple case like Freeda's the employer's burden is merely to "articulate" a legitimate, nondiscriminatory reason for his actions. The plaintiff then has the burden of "proving" that the employer's proffered reason was not the actual reason for the employment decision. In *Briggs,* the defendant's legitimate, nondiscriminatory reason for the wage disparity between nurses and sanitarians was that it was necessary to raise sanitarian wages, but not nurse wages, to recruit and to retain qualified employees. The plaintiffs in *Briggs* were then unable to prove that that was not the actual reason for the wage difference.

But the smoothness with which this allocation of burdens can be stated disguises its weaknesses. Should the employer be able to meet its burden by simply crying "market rates"? Or should the employer be required to show more, for example, that as a general practice it attempts to determine market rates before setting wages or that the market wage rates for nurses are indeed lower than those for sanitarians? Should market rates qualify at all as legitimate, nondiscriminatory reasons for wage disparities? Or are market rates so tainted by discrimination that they should not be available as a defense?

In summary, disparate treatment discrimination occurs when an employer acts with the intention of discriminating. But since direct evidence of intention is seldom available, the law specifies what evidence a plaintiff must present to create an inference of discriminatory intent and what evidence an employer must present to dispel such an inference. In simple cases, these inferences are quite reliable and, hence, most people accept them as reasonable. In complex cases, however, the inferences are less reliable. Since people disagree on their reasonableness, comparable worth litigation has been very controversial.

Disparate Impact Discrimination

Freeda Peeples applies for a job with a hospital. E.M. Ployer, the hospital's personnel director, decides to hire only people that weigh 180 pounds or more. Freeda weighs 100 pounds. She is not hired. Did E.M. Ployer discriminate?

E.M. Ployer's weight requirement presents a simple example of disparate impact discrimination. Employment criteria are illegal under this model of discrimination if they have an adverse effect on women and if they are not justified by business considerations. Freeda has the initial burden of identifying an employment criterion in use by the employer and proving that the criterion has an adverse effect on women. Here the employer is clearly using a weight requirement and, since women are generally smaller than men, Freeda should be able to prove that the requirement disqualifies a significantly higher proportion of women than men. If Freeda proves this adverse effect on women and no other evidence is presented, she has proven illegal discrimination. E.M. Ployer, however, has an opportunity to prove that the weight requirement is justified by business considerations. If E.M. can prove that one must weigh at least 180 pounds to perform the job duties in question, he has not engaged in disparate impact discrimination. The employer's intent to discriminate, which is the crux of disparate treatment discrimination, is irrelevant in disparate impact cases.[14] Freeda's ability to meet her initial burden depends wholly on the effect of the weight requirement on women as compared to men. And the employer's ability to meet its burden depends wholly on the extent to which the weight requirement is justified by the demands of the job in question.

The following case discusses how this model of discrimination applies to a comparable worth claim.

Spaulding v. University of Washington
740 F.2d 686 (9th Cir.),
cert. denied, 105 S.Ct. 511 (1984).

WALLACE, Circuit Judge:
Appellants are past and present members of the faculty of the University of Washington School of Nursing (the nursing faculty). In March 1972, members of the faculty of the School of Nursing filed a petition with Dr. Katz, Vice President for Academic Affairs and provost of the University, alleging sex discrimination by the University. The University responded to the petition and provided certain salary data. Dr. Grayson, Vice President of the Health Sciences Center, and Dr. Katz met with representatives of the nursing faculty to discuss the petition. The University asserted that salary levels varied because each academic discipline commanded a salary based upon training, expertise, emphasis, subject matter, and the academic marketplace for that discipline. Thus, the University argued that it was inappropriate to compare the average salary in one discipline with the composite average salary paid University faculty members. Subsequently, the University undertook, and made available to the nursing fac-

ulty, a more sophisticated study of salaries in the School of Nursing. The study concluded that faculty salaries as a whole at the University of Washington lagged 9 percent behind the salaries paid by schools with which the University had traditionally compared its salaries. The study also concluded that average faculty salaries in the School of Nursing lagged 10.9 percent behind salaries paid by comparable schools of nursing, but that many other disciplines also lagged at least that much behind.

The nursing faculty claims sex-based wage discrimination by the University in violation of Title VII of the Civil Rights Act of 1964. The nursing faculty argues that it presents a prima facie case of discrimination under the disparate impact theory. A showing of discriminatory animus is replaced under this theory by a showing of disproportionate impact, on a member of a group protected under Title VII, by an employer's facially neutral practice. Where applicable, the elements of a prima facie case under the most general formulation of the disparate impact model are: (1) the occurrence of certain outwardly neutral employment practices, and (2) a significantly adverse or disproportionate impact on persons of a particular sex produced by the employer's facially neutral acts or practices.

The nursing faculty's impact case is simply stated: they have shown a disparate impact by showing a wage disparity between only comparable jobs and this disparate impact is caused by the facially neutral policy or practice of the University of setting wages according to market prices for jobs in the disciplines. We confront then the difficult question whether the disparate impact model is available to plaintiffs who, as the nursing faculty here, make a broadranging sex-based claim of wage discrimination, based on comparable worth.

We hold that on facts such as these, where plaintiffs' sex-discrimination claim is a wide-ranging claim of wage disparity between only comparable jobs, the law does not go so far as to allow a prima facie case to be constructed by showing disparate impact. We so hold without making any broad statements as to the general availability of the impact model in other broad based sex-wage cases.

The case before us simply does not fit into the disparate impact model. The model was developed as a form of pretext analysis to handle specific employment practices not obviously job-related, such as: employers' intelligence tests which adversely affect minority persons, height and weight or other requirements affecting those of a certain sex, or policies which exclude applicants based on arrest records.

The nursing faculty unconvincingly cites cases for the proposition that "the disparate impact analysis has been applied to wage discrimination cases." They do not involve wide-ranging allegations challenging general wage policies but rather challenges to specific employer practices, namely, fringe benefits policies, with respect to which employers exercise judgment. The rules by which an employer determines the availability of fringe benefits can be evaluated in terms of their job-relatedness. It has been such selection procedures to which the disparate impact model has traditionally applied and not the mere payment of market wages.

We cannot manageably apply the impact model when the kernel of the plaintiff's theory is comparable worth. The problem is compounded in this case. When the disparate impact model is removed from the cases involving challenges to clearly delineated neutral policies of employers, it becomes so vague as to be inapplicable. The nursing faculty claims to have pinpointed a facially neutral policy at the University having the discriminatory impact they assert. That policy is the University's relying on the market to set their wages. We find that they have failed to do so, and emphasize that such a practice is not the sort of "policy" at which disparate impact analysis is aimed.

Relying on competitive market prices does not qualify as a facially neutral policy or practice for the purposes of disparate impact analysis. For Title VII purposes, simply labelling an employer's action a "policy or practice" is not sufficient. What matters is the substance of the employer's acts and whether those neutral acts are a non-job-related pretext to shield an invidious judgment.

Every employer constrained by market forces must consider market values in setting his labor costs. Naturally, market prices are inherently job-related, although the market may embody social judgments as to the worth of some jobs. Employers relying on the market are, to that extent, "price-takers." They deal with the market as a given, and do not meaningfully have a "policy" about it in the relevant Title VII sense. Fringe policies, whch are discretionary, are altogether another matter. Additionally, allowing plaintiffs to establish reliance on the market as a facially neutral policy for Title VII purposes would subject employers to liability for pay disparities with respect to which they have not, in any meaningful sense, made an independent business judgment. As we have previously said, "Title VII does not ultimately focus on ideal social distributions of persons of various races and both sexes. Instead it is concerned with combating culpable discrimination. In disparate impact cases, culpable discrimination takes the form of business decisions that have a discriminatory impact and are not justified by their job-relatedness."

[We hold that the disparate impact model of discrimination does not apply to this comparable worth claim.]

The plaintiffs in *Spaulding* attempted to fit their comparable worth claims into the disparate impact model. First, they identified an employment criterion in use by the employer. The university relied on wage rates in the marketplace to determine the wage rates for various job classifications within the university. The plaintiffs then claimed that they could prove that that criterion had an adverse impact on women. Since women and female-dominated occupations were paid less in the marketplace, use of the criterion would mean that women would be paid less by the university. Plaintiffs then argued that the burden should be on the university to prove that the use of market rates was required by business considerations.

The court in *Spaulding*, however, held that the disparate impact model was simply unavailable in comparable worth cases. The court said that only specific and discretionary criteria are susceptible to disparate impact attack and that the criterion relied upon in comparable worth cases—use of market wage rates—is neither specific nor discretionary. But what are specific and discretionary criteria and should they be used to limit disparate impact analysis?

Let us consider the specific criterion limitation first. Say that E.M. Ployer has established a hiring process that requires applicants to meet several requirements. Applicants must have a college degree, they must attain a certain score on a test administered by the hospital, they must submit acceptable references, and they must pass an interview with E.M. himself. The specific criterion limitation probably means that this process is not specific and, hence, not subject to disparate impact analysis. That is Freeda Peeples cannot prove discrimination by showing that the process has a disparate impact on women, for example, by showing that 50 percent of the men who apply eventually get jobs with the hospital, but only 10 percent of the women who apply eventually get jobs. Freeda could, however, use disparate impact analysis to attack a specific aspect of the process. She could, for example, prove that the test administered by the hospital was discriminatory by showing that 50 percent of male test-takers passed the test, but only 10 percent of female test-takers passed the test.

This analysis, however, fails to clarify the distinction between specific and nonspecific criteria. Let's say the test used by the hospital contains fifty questions. Is the test a specific criterion that is susceptible to disparate impact attack as the above analysis would suggest? Or do only individual questions qualify as specific criteria subject to attack? Moreover, if the analysis in the preceding paragraph is used to distinguish specific from nonspecific criteria, why was the use of market rates to set wages in *Spaulding* determined to be nonspecific? The university had a process for establishing the wages for each academic discipline that relied on a number of factors: training, expertise, emphasis, and subject matter, as well as the market rates for that discipline. Logically, if Freeda may challenge a specific aspect of the hiring process above, the plaintiffs in *Spaulding* should be able to challenge a specific aspect of the university's wage-setting process. If the use of market rates is not sufficiently specific, what more specific aspect of the use of market rates is susceptible to disparate impact analysis? In sum, without a theory and a method for distinguishing between specific and nonspecific criteria, the specific criterion limitation cannot be logically and consistently applied.

But let us assume for the moment that it is possible to distinguish between specific and nonspecific criterion. Why permit disparate impact analysis of specific criteria while prohibiting disparate impact analysis of nonspecific criteria? There are two primary rationales for this distinction.

The first rationale is that permitting plaintiffs to attack the use of nonspecific criteria would allow the disparate impact of one element of the hiring system to require validation of other elements having no adverse effects. To illustrate, assume that only one aspect of the hiring system used by E.M. Ployer, the test, had a disparate impact on women. The other aspects of the hiring system do not have a disparate impact on women, but because of the test, the system as a whole has a disparate impact. Thus, Freeda can prove that the hiring system has a disparate impact on women and the burden of proof would shift to E.M. Ployer to prove that the system is required by business necessity. The argument, then, is that permitting Freeda to attack the hiring system as a whole would require E.M. Ployer to prove the business necessity of the entire hiring process even though only one aspect of the process has a disparate impact on women. But the argument is upside down. One is certain when a system has a disparate impact that an element or a combination of elements of that system have a disparate impact. It is possible, although not necessary, that other elements of that system do not have a disparate impact. The exclusion of nonspecific criteria from disparate impact analysis, then, would permit the possible presence of innocent elements to immunize from attack other elements that certainly have a disparate impact. Rather than this anomaly, the disparate impact model should be treated as a burden-shifting device. Viewed in this way, a showing that a hiring system has a disparate impact does not necessarily require validation of every element of that system. Instead, the employer, who has greater access to the relevant information, bears the burden of isolating the elements of the system that create the disparate impact and of validating those elements. If the employer cannot isolate the elements causing the disparity, the burden will be on him to validate the system, but it is better to require the validation of innocent elements that may be present than to immunize discriminatory elements that are certainly present.

The specificity limitation is also supported by a manageability argument. The claim is that the model simply cannot be manageably applied when nonspecific employment criteria are attacked. But excluding nonspecific criteria from disparate impact analysis because of manageability problems is like eliminating mathematics from the curriculum because it is too difficult. Proving disparate impact and business necessity and finding appropriate remedies will be more difficult when nonspecific criteria are addressed, but that is not sufficient justification to immunize all nonspecific criteria from disparate impact attack.

Spaulding also held that the employer's practice of relying upon market rates to establish wage rates was not susceptible to disparate impact analysis because it was nondiscretionary. An employer setting wage rates must consider market rates and, in that context, is merely a passive price-taker. The court's theory was that one can only be liable for culpable discrimination and that one can only be culpable if one has sufficient discretion to avoid the objectionable conduct. In this context, the employer does not have such discretion because it would become noncompetitive if it failed to consider market wage rates. But this type of economic nondiscretion, assuming it exists, is a primary target of the antidiscrimination laws. An employer hiring only caucasian servers at a fast food outlet can claim economic discretion—that customers have a taste for discrimination and, hence, the outlet will be noncompetitive with discriminatory outlets if it hires black servers. But this type of nondiscretion, the same type relied upon in *Spaulding,* is not a defense to liability because all outlets are under a legal obligation not to compete through discrimination. Discretion, at least the type of economic discretion relied upon in *Spaulding,* should not be a prerequisite to disparate impact liability. Indeed, ironically, other judicial circuits have held that criteria must be nondiscretionary to be susceptible to disparate impact analysis.[15]

In summary, the *Spaulding* result is not likely to be the final word on the use of disparate impact theory in comparable worth cases. The two primary rationales supplied by the court are not supported by compelling logic. At the same time, however, comparable worth cases expose the problems of the disparate impact model and increase the urgency of either finding appropriate limitations or of otherwise dealing with the problems.

Comments and Perspective

Comparable worth litigation, and particularly litigation in the federal courts, has a very high national profile. The cases generally involve large sums of money and the media reports on them extensively. Litigation, however, is far from an ideal method of resolving comparable worth disputes. Its limitations are both practical and theoretical.

There are a number of practical shortcomings to comparable worth litigation. It is very slow. Simple comparable worth cases usually take years to resolve; complex cases may take a decade or more. Moreover, as this would indicate, litigation is very expensive. The expense of litigation creates several problems. First, money that could be used to resolve pay disparities goes instead to the lawyers and expert witnesses required by complex litigation. Second, the expense of this type of litigation places small employers and their employees in a peculiar position. On the one hand, small employers are practically immune from lawsuits dependent on the resources of their employees. The employees simply cannot afford it. Thus, small employers that engage in this type of discrimination may be able to avoid compliance with the law. On the other hand, because of the expense, the mere filing of a lawsuit endangers the financial stability of small employers, including those that are innocent of this type of discrimination. Third, the expense requires the parties to these lawsuits to seek allies. Employees, for example, might depend on unions or advocacy groups for financial assistance. As a result, the parties may lose an element of control over the lawsuits, which may make settlement more difficult, which may increase the total cost of the litigation, which requires the recruitment of more allies and results in a renewal of the inflationary cycle.

The complexity of comparable worth litigation also creates practical problems. It is a very rare judge, and even a rarer jury, that can understand all of the legal, economic, and social issues presented by the typical comparable worth case. This problem is aggravated by the structure of the courtroom, which consciously insulates the decision maker from experts who, if free discussion were allowed, might be able to enhance the decision maker's understanding.

Litigation also has theoretical limitations as a mechanism for resolving comparable worth lawsuits. Comparable worth is a social problem that, in an ideal world, demands a broad response. Litigation, however, is by its nature very limited. A lawsuit is brought against only one of many employers, all of whom hire people in female-dominated occupations and pay them the market rate. Is it just to hold one employer liable for a wrong in which many indulge?

Moreover, even if litigation leads to broad change, it may not be the ideal process for creating that change. In a democracy, the ideal process for resolving a social problem is the democratic process. Litigation is not a democratic process; indeed, the judiciary is structured so that it can withstand majoritarian pressures. Although the judiciary may be an appropriate instrument for change if the democratic process is flawed (if black persons, for example, are prohibited from participating equally in the democratic process), it is far from clear that that is the situation with the comparable worth issue.[16] The disadvantaged group—women—is both politically active and a majority of the population.

Despite these limitations, litigation will undoubtedly continue to be a major response to comparable worth disputes. Perhaps that means nothing more than that we are not living in an ideal world. Litigation, in this area as in many others, is a response of last resort. Even though comparable worth claims have been uniformly rejected by the federal courts, increasing numbers of cases are filed each year.[17] Moreover, as we will see in the next chapter, there are several as yet unused litigation arrows in the state law quiver that are likely to be used as the federal law quiver empties. Perhaps this is another testament to the American propensity to litigate.[18] When other avenues do not promise prompt redress, Americans litigate.

3
Comparable Worth Legislation

T he comparable worth drama is being played on a national stage, but there are a number of state and local actors. The major state initiatives to date have focused on state employees. Six states are currently implementing programs designed to equalize pay levels between male-dominated and female-dominated jobs and two dozen other states have established task forces to study the issue. In addition to these initiatives for state employees, some states have enacted comparable worth laws that extend to the private sector. This chapter first discusses comparable worth and state employees, then it considers state laws requiring comparable worth in the private sector, and finally it summarizes the legislative response to comparable worth.

Comparable Worth and Public Employees

Describing state efforts to implement comparable worth for public employees is like trying to describe the position of ants on an anthill—by the time you've described them, they've moved. The value of the description, then, lies not in the position of individual states at any particular point in time, but in the developing trends—in the slowly emerging shape of the anthill. This section describes the position of individual states and, in so doing, provides a glimpse of the anthill under construction.[1]

State efforts to implement comparable worth for public employees generally occur in three stages. First, a task force is established to gather information about the earnings gap between male and female state employees and about the extent of sex segregation in state employment; second, a professional job evaluation is authorized and completed; and, third, a process is established and money is appropriated to rectify any pay imbalances that have been identified. A few states have completed all these stages, others have completed one or two, and still others have not yet addressed the comparable worth issue.

Data Collection

More than half of the states have established task forces of one sort or another to study the issue of comparable worth.[2] The mission of these task forces is to collect data on the work and wages of male and female state employees. The information then provides a basis for the more detailed and expensive professional job evaluation.

The task forces have been organized in three basic ways. The task forces in Massachusetts and New York will study the comparable worth issue as part of a general review of the state's compensation scheme.[3] The task forces in most states, though, have been organized to consider the comparable worth issue only and are composed of representatives from various interested groups, such as women's advocacy groups, unions, state personnel administrators, and so forth. Finally, in some states the task forces have been authorized to employ a professional job evaluator. (Professional job evaluation will be discussed later in this chapter.)

This movement towards a consideration of the comparable worth issue, however, is not unanimous. Ten states have rejected bills to establish comparable worth task forces,[4] a number of states have not yet taken any action on the issue,[5] and two states have suspended operation of their task forces.[6] Why should there be this reluctance to gather the data upon which a sound public policy can be based? Studying the issue, after all, does not commit the state to any particular resolution of the issue or, indeed, to any resolution at all.

This reluctance has been caused in part by the highly publicized comparable worth case from Washington state, *AFSCME v. State of Washington*.[7] In Washington, the state authorized a preliminary study of wage disparities in 1973 and a study by a professional job evaluator in 1974. Both studies revealed significant pay disparities between male-dominated and female-dominated jobs, disparities that were not attributable to job content. The legislature, however, failed to rectify the imbalances. In *AFSCME*, a federal district judge, relying in part on the legislature's failure to rectify the imbalances its studies had revealed, held that the state had violated the federal employment discrimination laws. Although the decision was later overturned on appeal, estimates of the state's back pay liability at the time ranged as high as $500 million. The message of *AFSCME* to states contemplating data collection was that comparable worth studies lead to litigation.

Despite that reading of *AFSCME*, it is not true that comparable worth studies by states increase the likelihood of comparable worth lawsuits. Potential beneficiaries of comparable worth lawsuits, as well as everyone else, prefer that these types of problems be resolved short of litigation. As was discussed in chapter 2, litigation is time-consuming and expensive. If a comparable worth study were commenced, persons who might otherwise file a lawsuit would be likely to wait in the belief or the hope that the perceived problems could be resolved without litigation. On the other hand, if a study is not commenced, litigation would be at or near the top of the list of alternatives for potential beneficiaries. In the short run, then, a comparable worth study should decrease, rather than increase, the likelihood of a comparable worth lawsuit.

The effect of a study in the long run is subject to many uncertainties. If the study demonstrates pay equity in the state personnel system, obviously the likelihood of a comparable worth lawsuit would decrease. If the study uncovers inequities, the legislature will have to decide whether to rectify them. If the legislature decides to rectify the inequities, once again the likelihood of a comparable worth lawsuit would decrease. If the legislature decides not to rectify the inequities, potential plantiffs may file a lawsuit. Such plaintiffs would be in a more advantageous position than they would have been in without a comparable worth study because they will be able to rely upon the study to some extent in the litigation. The state, however, will also enter the poststudy litigation with an advantage; the state will have avoided back pay liability for a period of time equal to the time between when a lawsuit would have been filed without a study and when a lawsuit was filed with the study. In *AFSCME*, this period of time may have been as long as six years. In the long run, then, there are three possible outcomes. If the study demonstrates pay equity or if the study discloses pay inequities and the legislature acts to rectify them, the likelihood of a comparable worth lawsuit would decrease. If the study discloses inequities and the legislature fails to act, the study would provide advantages to potential plaintiffs in a lawsuit, but it would also provide advantages to the state.

Job Evaluation

The term job evaluation refers to formal procedures for comparing jobs. Job evaluations have become an important part of the comparable worth debate because of the way in which they are used to create an inference of sex discrimination. In *Briggs v. City of Madison*, a case discussed in chapter 2, the court held that an inference of sex discrimination could be established by demonstrating that a female-dominated job classification was paid less than a male-dominated job classification where the two job classifications were very similar in skill, effort, responsibility, and working conditions. In most cases, plaintiffs rely on a job evaluation study to establish that the two job classifications are similar in skill, effort, responsibility, and working conditions. Thus, if male- and female-dominated jobs are determined to be comparable by a job evaluation study and the female-dominated job is paid less, the inference is that the difference in pay is the result of sex discrimination and, therefore, is illegal.

Job evaluations have also become important outside of the litigation context. Ten states have authorized professional job evaluations to assess the extent of sex bias in public employment.[8] Once again, the job evaluation is used to determine whether male- and female-dominated jobs that are paid differently are comparable in skill, effort, responsibility, and working conditions. If they are, the inference is that the difference in pay is attributable to sex discrimination and should be remedied.

Given these uses of job evaluation studies, job evaluation methodology is quite important.[9] An inference of sex discrimination can only be as valid and reliable as the job evaluation study upon which it is based. The central principle of job evaluation is that it is the job, not the worker, that is evaluated. Although there are a number of different job evaluation systems, all follow a common basic methodology. First, each job to be evaluated is carefully observed and described. Then each job is evaluated and rated upon a common scale. It is this evaluation and rating which primarily distinguishes the various job evaluation systems. Finally, the evaluation and rating derived from the job evaluation are used to set or revise wage and salary levels.

There are four basic job evaluation systems. The ranking and classification methods are qualitative and the factor comparison and point methods are quantitative. Although all four methods are briefly described, the point method is emphasized here because it is by far the most popular of the methods.[10]

The Ranking Method. In the ranking method, jobs are simply ranked from highest to lowest in terms of "worth" or "value" to the firm. Usually either a card-sorting or a paired-comparison procedure is used to accomplish the ranking. In the card-sorting procedure, evaluators are simply provided with cards that identify each job to be ranked and are asked to rank the jobs from highest to lowest by sorting the cards. In the paired-comparison procedure, the evaluators compare each job with every other job so that each job earns a score based on how often it is deemed more important. Generally, neither procedure provides a definition of worth or value (or, if one is provided, it is very amorphous), so evaluators must rely on their own notions of those concepts to accomplish the ranking.

The ranking method is simple and, hence, relatively easy to apply if there are not a large number of jobs to compare. The method, however, is unwieldy with large numbers of jobs. With the paired-comparison procedure, for example, 45 comparisons must be made if there are 10 jobs to be ranked, but 1,225 comparisons must be made with 50 jobs and 4,950 comparisons must be made with 100 jobs. Moreover, since the evaluators must be familiar with every job rated, it becomes increasingly more difficult to find qualified evaluators as the number of jobs increases. The ranking method also has other shortcomings. Since the method provides no measure of value, the addition of a new job or a change in duties in an existing job may require the entire evaluation procedure to be redone. Finally, the most troublesome aspect of the method is the extreme subjectivity caused by the lack of clearly defined and objective criteria for comparing jobs. Because of these problems, and others, the ranking method is not well-respected by professional job evaluators and is not of much utility in comparable worth cases.[11]

The Classification Method. In the classification method, job levels are predetermined and described in terms of factors such as skill, effort, and responsibility. Then each job is evaluated and placed in the most appropriate job level. A classification system might, for example, establish fifteen job levels. Job level 1 might be defined to include jobs with no latitude for the exercise of independent judgment, job level 2 to include jobs with limited latitude for independent judgment, and so forth. Each job would then be evaluated and placed at the most appropriate level. The General Schedule (GS) classification used by the United States Civil Service Commission is the best known classification system. It uses eight factors to define eighteen job or "GS" levels; every job in the system is evaluated and assigned a GS level for pay purposes.

The classification method, like the ranking method, is relatively easy to implement. The method, though, is unreliable. The placement of particular jobs into job levels depends to a large extent on evaluator expertise and, hence, is subject to biases and inconsistencies. This is especially true where a job ranks high on one factor but low on another, for example, where a job requires high educational levels but does not involve supervisory responsibilities.[12]

The Factor Comparison Method. The factor comparison method requires several steps. First, four to seven "compensable" factors, such as skill, effort, and responsibility, are chosen. Second, a number of "benchmark" jobs are selected. The benchmark jobs should be selected so that a consensus can be reached regarding their relative worth. To illustrate, let us assume that secretary and messenger are selected as the benchmark jobs.[13] Third, each benchmark job is analyzed to determine the extent to which each of the compensable factors contributes to the total worth of the job. Thus, if secretaries are paid $200 per week, it might be determined that $100 is attributable to skill, $70 to responsibility, and $30 to effort, and if messengers are paid $100 per week, it might be determined that $10 is attributable to skill, $40 to responsibility, and $50 to effort. Finally, each job in the organization is compared to the benchmark jobs factor by factor, so that the total of the compensable factors equals the value for the particular job.

The factor comparison method is not widely used for several reasons: the method is very time-consuming to execute; it is difficult to explain to employees; the selection of benchmark jobs may heavily influence the results, but no clear guides are provided for their selection; and the assignment of money values to compensable factors has no theoretical or statistical justification.[14]

The Point Method. The point method, also called the point factor method, is the most widely used of the major methods of job evaluation. In the point method, the first step is the selection of a set of evaluation factors. The most common factors, once again, are skill, effort, responsibility, and working conditions, but these broad factors may be subdivided into narrower categories. Each factor is then assigned a maximum number of points (a "weight"), which is intended to reflect the importance of the factor in relation to other factors. Skill, for example, might be given a weight of 200 and working conditions a weight of 50. "Degrees" are also defined for each factor. A degree is the relative amount of a factor that a particular job requires. The higher the degree, the higher the number of points a job would receive on a particular factor. The factors and their weight and degrees can either be determined *a priori* or empirically. If an *a priori* approach is used, the evaluators use factors, weights, and degrees that they believe to be relevant and legitimate. If an empirical approach is used, the evaluators use statistics (generally multiple regression analysis) to determine which factors, weights, and degrees best predict the existing wage structure for selected jobs and then apply those factors, weights, and degrees to all jobs. This is often called a "policy capturing" approach because it makes explicit the policies underlying the existing wage structure.[15] Once the factors, weights, and degrees have been determined, each job is first described and then rated on each factor separately and assigned the appropriate number of points. The points received by a job on each factor are then totaled to yield the overall score for the job.

Several concerns are raised by the use of the point method of job evaluation in comparable worth settings.[16] To illustrate, assume that an employer uses the point method to evaluate jobs and that job A and job B both earn 25 points. (See figure 3–1.) Also assume that job A is male-dominated and paid more than job B, a female-dominated job. Comparable worth proponents would argue that sex discrimination has been shown on the basis of the job evaluation and that, as a result, a remedy is appropriate.

One concern with this result involves reliability. Is the point method of job evaluation sufficiently reliable to support claims of sex discrimination? Reliability is consistency; does the method yield the same results on successive trials? Thus, if the point method yielded 25 points for jobs A and B every time the jobs were analyzed, it would be reliable. If, however, it yielded different results on successive trials, the point method would be unreliable; the results on some trials would necessarily be invalid and, hence, any findings of sex discrimination based on the method would be questionable.[17] There are a number of reasons to doubt the reliability of the point method. First, the selection of factors and factor weights may vary from trial to trial, especially if the *a priori* approach is used for selection. Differences in factors and factor weights can have very substantial consequences on the ultimate ranking of jobs.[18] Second, the description of jobs may lead to variability between trials. The job descriptions are usually based on information supplied by supervisors. That information is only as valid as the supervisors' awareness of job duties; a law school dean, for example, may be quite aware of the job duties of a faculty member, but only dimly aware of all of the duties of a secretary. Even if the information is solid, however, a great deal of subjective judgment is involved in selecting important tasks and duties to be included in the job description and in omitting minor responsibilities. Third, there may be variability in the assessment of jobs once they have been described. A great deal of judgment is involved in determining where to rank a job on a particular factor. The few studies that have been completed on the reliability of job evaluation methods tend to confirm these doubts.[19]

Another concern with the use of the point method in comparable worth settings is validity. Validity refers to the extent to which a test (the point method of job evaluation in this case) accurately measures the reality that it is designed to assess.[20] Validity is a particularly difficult issue in this context because the point method is designed to assess a reality that is not easily defined or verifiable. This type of validity is called construct validity because the reality being measured is a construct—an unobservable, postulated reality.

There is no consensus on the construct that the point method is designed to measure. Some commentators contend that the construct has not been adequately defined,[21] while others propose various definitions such as job value or worth,[22] job content and difficulty,[23] and compensable cultural values in the marketplace.[24] There is consensus, though, that the construct, however defined, excludes the effect of sex on the ultimate ranking of jobs. As a result, if the point method in measuring the construct fails to exclude the influence of sex on job rank, it is not valid. There are two principal ways in which job rank under the point system may be affected by sex. First, the evaluation of jobs may be affected by sex role stereotypes. A number of studies in experimental social psychology have demonstrated that women workers are evaluated less favorably than male workers. In these studies, subjects are presented with identical descriptions of workers, except that some workers are identified as male and some as female, and asked to evaluate the workers on some scale. Except in one relatively narrow circumstance,[25] female workers are rated less favorably than male workers even though they have identical characteristics.[26] If this same phenomenon affects the evaluation of jobs, and there is some evidence to believe that it does,[27] female-dominated jobs may be rated less favorably than male-dominated jobs because the jobs are associated with female workers.[28] Second, the selection of factors,

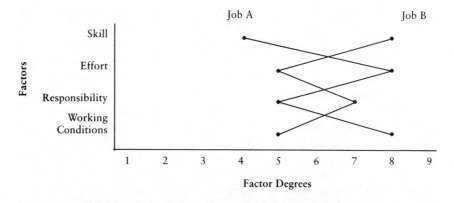

Figure 3–1. Rankings on a Hypothetical Job Evaluation

weights, and degrees may introduce a sex bias. If an empirical approach is used for selection, the evaluators use statistics to determine which factors, weights, and degrees best predict the existing wage structure for selected jobs and then apply those factors, weights, and degrees to all jobs. But, of course, if the existing wage structure has a sex bias (and one of the central tenets of comparable worth proponents is that it does), this process incorporates that bias into the point method of job evaluation. If an *a priori* approach is used for selection, evaluators use factors, weights, and degrees that they believe to be relevant and legitimate. But, once again, if the experimental social psychology studies are valid, evaluators may be influenced in making their selections by the extent to which certain factors are associated with male or female work. These criticisms weaken the inference of sex discrimination created by the point method in comparable worth cases. If the point method is not a valid method for ranking jobs because the sex of incumbents affects the rankings, the point method is *a fortiori* not a valid method for detecting sex discrimination in wage structures.

The logic underlying the use of the point method in comparable worth settings raises another set of concerns. For the hypothetical situation based on figure 3–1, the logic of comparable worth proponents could be articulated as follows: (1) job A is paid more than job B, (2) the difference in pay is not attributable to job duties because the point method of job evaluation ranks the jobs equally, (3) job A is male dominated and job B is female dominated; (4) therefore, the difference in pay must be attributable to sex discrimination. The conclusion of sex discrimination is troublesome because it does not necessarily follow from the premises. The difference in pay may be attributable to other factors. For example, the workers in job A, but not job B, may be unionized or may possess skills that are in great demand in the labor market.

1,800 job classifications. The study found that female-dominated job clas-sifications were paid, on average, 25 percent less than comparable male-dominated job classifications. For example, the study found that registered nurses and vocational education instructors ranked equally under the job evaluation system, but the nurses, 94 percent of whom were women, earned a maximum of $1,723 per month, while the all male instructors earned a maximum of $2,260 per month.

In 1982, the Minnesota legislature acted on the study. It enacted a statute that established a comparable worth policy and a procedure for implement-ing that policy. The comparable worth policy reads as follows:

> It is the policy of this state to attempt to establish equitable compensation relationships between female-dominated, male-dominated, and balanced classes of employees in the executive branch. Compensation relationships are equitable . . . when the primary consideration in negotiating, establish-ing, recommending, and approving total compensation is comparability of the value of the work in relationship to other positions in the executive branch.[32]

The procedure for implementing the policy was first used in 1983. In January of odd-numbered years, the Commissioner of Employee Relations submits to the legislature a list of female-dominated classifications that are paid less than other classifications with the same number of job evaluation points. The Minnesota Legislative Commission on Employee Relations then recommends to the appropriate legislative committees an amount to be ap-propriated for pay equity adjustments. In 1983, the legislature acted on the recommendation and approved a biennial appropriation of $21.8 million. The funds could be used only for salary equalization and if they were not so used they would revert back to the state treasury. The funds were adminis-tratively assigned to bargaining units, so the actual distribution of increases was negotiated through the collective bargaining process.

In the 1983–1985 biennium about 8,000 employees in 151 job classifi-cations received pay equity adjustments averaging about $1,600 each. If an amount similar to that appropriated in 1983 is appropriated in 1985, the program should be fully implemented for state employees by 1987. At that time, the pay equity raises would constitute about 4 percent of the state's total payroll costs.

In 1984, the Minnesota legislature acted to extend the pay equity pro-gram to local governments, to cities, counties, and school districts. The Local Government Pay Equity Act requires each local government to establish eq-uitable compensation relationships among female-dominated, male-domi-nated and balanced classes of employees. The law uses the same definition of "equitable compensation relationships" as the law for state employees. The law requires local governments to use a job evaluation system to compare the value of various job classifications. The governments can either develop their own system or borrow one used by another public employer in the state.

As an incentive to comply, the law also provides local governments with certain protections. The state human rights department and state courts are prohibited from using data from any job evaluation in a discrimination suit that commences before August 1, 1987. Thus, the prospect of costly litigation should not dissuade local governments from actively complying with the law. Until 1987, their compliance activities will not expose them to a greater risk of state litigation. After 1987, local governments that in good faith attempt to comply with the law should obtain some measure of protection from litigation through their very efforts and, if they are sued, their ultimate liability should be minimized to some extent. Local governments that do not attempt to comply, however, will be particularly vulnerable to lawsuits because the very data that they are required to compile may be used against them.

In summary, then, Minnesota has done the most to implement pay equity for public employees. The Minnesota laws affecting state and local governmental employees apply to about 10 percent of the entire Minnesota workforce. Moreover, although there have been attempts to limit the scope of the Local Government Pay Equity Act, the implementation has proceeded relatively smoothly.

Comparable Worth and Private Employers

All but four states have employment discrimination laws that apply to private sector employers.[33] These laws, like the federal laws they are based on, take two general forms. First, there are broad "fair employment practices" laws that, like Title VII of the Civil Rights Act of 1964, use general language to forbid employers from discriminating on the basis of sex.[34] Second, there are relatively narrow "equal pay" laws that, like the Equal Pay Act of 1963, require employers to pay equal wages for equal work.[35] Most states have both types of laws.[36] Fifteen of the state employment discimination laws, however, are considerably broader than the federal laws because they require private employers to pay men and women equally for comparable work. (See table 3–1.) While two of the fifteen laws have no enforcement mechanisms and, hence, are merely hortatory, thirteen impose enforceable obligations on private sector employers. This section discusses the thirteen state employment discrimination laws that create comparable worth obligations.[37]

No federal law explicitly requires equal pay for comparable work.[38] The Equal Pay Act requires equal pay only if men and women are doing the same work. Thus, if an employer pays male nurses more than female nurses, the Equal Pay Act is violated, but the Equal Pay Act is not violated if the employer pays male janitors more than female nurses. Consequently, the Equal Pay Act is not of much use in comparable worth cases where the claim is that male-dominated jobs are unjustifiably paid more than different, but comparable, female-dominated jobs.

Federal comparable worth cases are generally brought under Title VII. Title VII, with broad statutory language, prohibits employers from discriminating on the basis of sex. The plaintiff has the initial burden of creating an inference of sex discrimination. In comparable worth cases, the plaintiff generally attempts to do this by proving that the employer pays a female-dominated job less than a male-dominated job for work that is comparable in skill, effort, and responsibility. A few courts have held that this type of proof is sufficient to prove a prima facie [39] violation of Title VII.[40] Most courts, however, have held that this type of proof is not sufficient to prove a prima facie violation of Title VII and would require additional, albeit unspecified, evidence of sex discrimination.[41] If a plaintiff proves a prima facie violation of Title VII by creating an inference of sex discrimination, the employer then has the burden of articulating a legitimate, nondiscriminatory reason for the pay differential. The employer's burden is quite light at this stage. The employer need not prove that there is a legitimate, nondiscriminatory reason for the pay differential; he must merely articulate one. Thus, in *Briggs v. City of Madison* the employer said that his reliance on market wage rates explained the wage differential between male- and female-dominated jobs.[42] The employer did not have to prove that the market rate for the male job was higher than the market rate for the female job, or that he generally relied on market rates in setting wage levels. Merely articulating the reason was sufficient to meet the employer's burden. To prevail, the plaintiff must then prove that the employer's articulated reason—in *Briggs,* reliance on market wage rates— was not the true reason for the wage differential.

In a number of respects, the state comparable wage laws are much more favorable to plaintiffs than Title VII. The state laws generally provide that no employer shall discriminate by paying any employee a wage rate less than the rate he pays to any employee of the opposite sex for comparable work. Thus, under the state laws, a plaintiff can clearly establish a prima facie case by proving that an employer pays a female-dominated job less than a male-dominated job that requires comparable work.[43] In contrast, under Title VII, the courts are split on the elements necessary to establish a prima facie case. Moreover, unlike Title VII, many of the state laws provide guidance on how to prove comparable work by delineating the job characteristics to be compared. (See table 3–1.) In North Dakota and South Dakota, for example, the male- and female-dominated jobs must be comparable on skill, effort, and responsibility, but not on physical strength. As a result, if a job evaluation rated male- and female-dominated jobs equally except that the male-dominated job required greater physical strength, it would be clear in North and

Table 3–1
Characteristics of State Comparable Worth Laws Applicable to Private Sector Employers

	AK[a]	AR[b]	GA[c]	ID[d]	KY[e]	ME[f]	MD[g]	MA[h]	NE[i]	ND[j]	OK[k]	OR[l]	SD[m]	TN[n]	WV[o]
Requirement contained in:															
State equal pay law		•	•	•	•	•	•	•	•	•	•	•	•	•	•
State fair employment practices law	•														
Enforceable	•	•		•	•	•	•	•		•	•	•	•	•	•
Hortatory only			•						•						
Characteristics compared:															
Not enumerated	•	•					•	•							
Skill, effort, and responsibility				•	•	•									
Skill, effort and responsibility but not physical strength										•	•		•		
Other												•[p]		•[q]	•[p]
Affirmative defenses:															
Seniority		•		•	•	•	•	•		•	•	•	•	•	•
Merit system				•	•	•	•			•	•	•	•	•	•

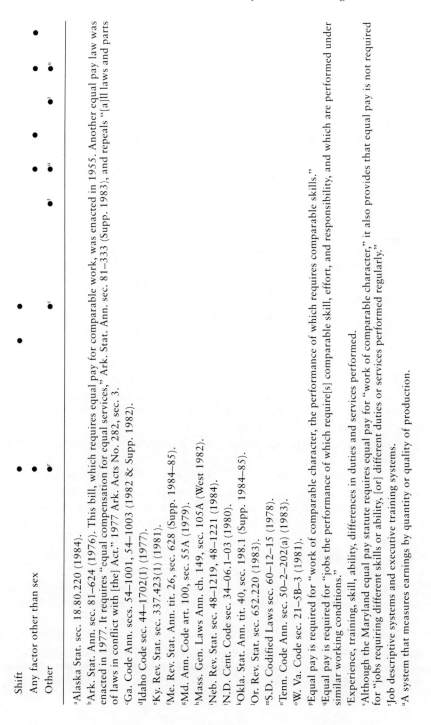

Shift							
Any factor other than sex							
Other							

[a] Alaska Stat. sec. 18.80.220 (1984).

[b] Ark. Stat. Ann. sec. 81–624 (1976). This bill, which requires equal pay for comparable work, was enacted in 1955. Another equal pay law was enacted in 1977. It requires "equal compensation for equal services," Ark. Stat. Ann. sec. 81–333 (Supp. 1983), and repeals "[a]ll laws and parts of laws in conflict with [the] Act." 1977 Ark. Acts No. 282, sec. 3.

[c] Ga. Code Ann. secs. 54–1001, 54–1003 (1982 & Supp. 1982).

[d] Idaho Code sec. 44–1702(1) (1977).

[e] Ky. Rev. Stat. sec. 337.423(1) (1981).

[f] Me. Rev. Stat. Ann. tit. 26, sec. 628 (Supp. 1984–85).

[g] Md. Ann. Code art. 100, sec. 55A (1979).

[h] Mass. Gen. Laws Ann. ch. 149, sec. 105A (West 1982).

[i] Neb. Rev. Stat. sec. 48–1219, 48–1221 (1984).

[j] N.D. Cent. Code sec. 34–06.1–03 (1980).

[k] Okla. Stat. Ann. tit. 40, sec. 198.1 (Supp. 1984–85).

[l] Or. Rev. Stat. sec. 652.220 (1983).

[m] S.D. Codified Laws sec. 60–12–15 (1978).

[n] Tenn. Code Ann. sec. 50–2–202(a) (1983).

[o] W. Va. Code sec. 21–5B–3 (1981).

[p] Equal pay is required for "work of comparable character, the performance of which requires comparable skills."

[q] Equal pay is required for "jobs the performance of which require[s] comparable skill, effort, and responsibility, and which are performed under similar working conditions."

[r] Experience, training, skill, ability, differences in duties and services performed.

[s] Although the Maryland equal pay statute requires equal pay for "work of comparable character," it also provides that equal pay is not required for "jobs requiring different skills or ability, [or] different duties or services performed regularly."

[t] Job descriptive systems and executive training systems.

[u] A system that measures earnings by quantity or quality of production.

South Dakota, but not under Title VII, that the jobs were comparable for comparable worth purposes.

The state laws are also more favorable to plaintiffs than Title VII because of two aspects of the employer's burden once a prima facie case has been presented. First, the employer must satisfy a higher level of proof to meet his burden under the state laws. Under Title VII, the employer need only articulate a legitimate, nondiscriminatory reason for the wage disparity to satisfy his burden. Under all but one of the state laws,[44] the employer must prove that the wage disparity is justified by one of the specified affirmative defenses.[45] As a result, once a prima facie case has been presented by the plaintiff, the employer may satisfy his burden under Title VII by merely asserting that differences in seniority explain the wage differential between male- and female-dominated jobs. To prevail, the plaintiff would than have to prove that seniority differences did not explain the differential. To satisfy his burden under the state laws, the employer would have to prove, not merely assert, that seniority differences explained the wage differential. Second, many of the state laws are more favorable to plaintiffs because they limit employers to certain relatively narrow defenses. Under Title VII, employers have an infinite variety of defenses available to them; wage differentials between male- and female-dominated jobs are legal under Title VII if they are caused by a seniority system, a merit system, a system that measures earnings by quantity or quality of production, or *any other factor other than sex*. Many of the state laws provide only a few defenses. In Massachusetts, the employer can meet his burden only by demonstrating that the wage differential is based on seniority, while in Idaho and Kentucky only seniority and merit system defenses are recognized. (See table 3–1.)

Despite these significant advantages to plaintiffs, no comparable worth cases have been litigated under these state laws. One reason for this may be that the laws are not what they seem. The laws are not modern and it may be that comparable work was intended to mean something quite different when the laws were enacted. But even if this argument were persuasive, and the proponent would bear a heavy burden to overcome the plain language of the statute, it does not explain the failure to test the statutes. Most litigation is commenced without a certainty of success, and much litigation, certainly in the area of employment discrimination, is commenced primarily to explore the potential of a statute or line of argument. The answer may depend more on the states in which these statutes are found. They are not states, for the most part, that are at the forefront of the comparable worth effort. They are not Minnesota, Washington, or California. They are instead smaller, perhaps less progressive, states where the resources to mount risky litigation efforts and to disseminate the results of those efforts are more limited. The statutes do, however, provide a significant, but currently unexplored, litigation opportunity for plaintiffs.

Comments and Perspective

Legislation is a term that, generally defined, encompasses broad rules designed to govern large numbers of people. Litigation, in contrast, is the application of those rules to individuals or to relatively small numbers of people. Given this definition, it is clear that there is a great deal of comparable worth legislation, but it is confined to a relatively narrow field.

There is widespread experimentation with comparable worth legislation in the states. Most states have enacted some type of legislation relating to public employees and some states have legislation that extends to private employers. Every region of the country has states with such legislation. An advantage of this decentralization is that a number of different approaches to the issue are being tried. Some states, like Minnesota, appear to be satisfied with their legislation; others, like North Carolina, are dissatisfied. All of the approaches, however, will provide guidance to those considering legislation in the future.

Legislation at the state level, though, is only one type of legislation that might be used to address the comparable worth issue. Federal and private legislation have been slow in coming. At the federal level, the disparity between male and female pay mirrors that in the private sector. A recent study of 2.1 million full-time federal workers by the General Accounting Office found that women on average were paid 63 percent of what men were paid. The General Accounting Office, however, urged caution in studying the reasons for the disparity and in taking steps to rectify that portion of the disparity that is unexplained by economic factors.[46] The Congress, exercising more than caution, has failed to pass bills in recent sessions that would have authorized studies of pay disparities between male and female federal workers, as well as other bills relating to the comparable worth issue.

Private legislation has also been slow in coming. In the private sector, broad rules designed to cover large numbers of people generally take the form of collective bargaining agreements. But few inroads have been made on the issue in private sector collective bargaining agreements.[47] The primary reason for this appears to be the almost uniform opposition to the comparable worth concept by corporations, although the extent to which most unions are male dominated may also play a role.

In summary, there is a wealth of experience with comparable worth legislation, most of it involving public employees at the state level. There is also a modicum of experience with comparable worth legislation that is directed at private sector employers, also at the state level. Legislation at the federal and private levels on the comparable worth issue, however, has been slow in coming.

4

Comparable Worth in Other Countries

The economic conditions that gave rise to comparable worth theory in the United States—wage disparities between males and females and job segregation—are also present in virtually every other Western industrialized country. As tables 4–1 and 4–2 illustrate, the difference between the countries is not in the presence or absence of the conditions, but in the extent of the wage disparities and segregation. It is not surprising, then, that the United States is not alone in developing a comparable worth jurisprudence. It is surprising, though, that the literature on comparable worth in the United States refers so sparingly to the experience of other countries.

There are several explanations for the insularity of the United States on this issue. First, the United States was the first major country to enact employment discrimination laws and its experiences greatly influenced the development of discrimination jurisprudence in other countries. The perception in the United States is that we are still on the cutting edge and that other countries are looking to us for ideas and directions. That, however, is no longer true, especially on the comparable worth issue. In the United Kingdom, for example, the influence of American jurisprudence was very strong when employment discrimination laws were first enacted in the early 1970s, but the country's reliance on American precedent has waned considerably since 1980 and, on the comparable worth issue, the country has charted a course considerably different from that in the United States. Another reason for the insularity of the United States is the sheer size of the American judicial system. It is more than a full-time job to stay current with the developments in the United States, let alone venture into the unknown wilds of another country's experiments. Smaller, less diverse countries must look to lessons learned in other countries to develop their law; in the United States, one can find new approaches in other judicial districts, other states, or other municipalities. Finally, insularity finds explanation in the culture of the United States. The study of foreign languages and history is not highly valued in America. Comparative law is not required study in any American law school.

Despite these reasons for its existence, the insularity of the United States

Table 4–1
Female Earnings as a Percentage of Male Earnings in Selected Industrialized Countries, 1981[a]

Country	Percentage
Australia	80.4
Canada	63.6
New Zealand	71.6
Sweden	90.1
United Kingdom	68.8
United States	59.2

Sources: Adapted from International Labour Office, *Women at Work*, no. 1 (Geneva: International Labour Office, 1983), 5; Statistics Canada, Social and Economic Studies Division, *Women in Canada A Statistical Report* (Ottawa: Minister of Supply & Services Canada, 1985), 61; U.S. Department of Labor, *Time of Change: 1983 Handbook on Women Workers* (Washington, D.C.: U.S. Government Printing Office, 1983), 82.

[a]Because of differences in methodologies and data bases, strict comparisons between countries should not be made on the basis of these statistics.

Table 4–2
Occupational Sex Segregation in Selected Industrialized Countries[a]

	Managers			Laborers			Clericals		
	Male	Female	Percent	Male	Female	Percent	Male	Female	Percent
	(in thousands)		Male	*(in thousands)*		Male	*(in thousands)*		Female
Australia	290	45	87	1,853	254	88	329	750	70
Canada	800	366	69	2,712	446	86	386	1,506	80
New Zealand	42	4	91	391	67	85	67	148	69
Sweden	76	19	80	1,040	223	82	101	429	81
United States	7,063	3,070	70	24,601	5,852	81	3,854	12,997	77

Source: Adapted from International Labour Office, *Yearbook of Labour Statistics* (Geneva: International Labour Office, 1984), table 2B, 106–49.

Note: The United Kingdom was not included in the ILO survey.

[a]Because of differences in methodologies and data bases, strict comparisons between countries should not be made on the basis of these statistics.

on the comparable worth issue is unfortunate. An awareness of the experiences of other countries helps us to assess our own experience. Concepts that we have accepted as fundamental may be more correctly perceived as historical and cultural adaptations if other countries have made progress with quite different concepts. Corrective measures that seem essential may seem less so if some countries have failed with those measures and others have succeeded with quite different measures. The deeply ingrained myths and the unstated premises of our system may only be perceptible from the vantage point of another country. But a comparative perspective does more than improve the view. One encounters a sense of uncertainty when examining the laws and social structures of another country; the complexities and nuances cannot be fully understood, relevant considerations may be overlooked. But this sense of uncertainty is the key to learning and, eventually, to understanding. If, once rearmed with uncertainty, one looks again at one's own country, new questions and perspectives may challenge the old orthodoxies.

Ironically, then, this examination of the experiences of other countries is merely a continuation of the search for an understanding of the experience of the United States. It is not a search for solutions that can be transplanted because what works well in New Zealand or Sweden may not, indeed probably will not, work well in the United States. Instead, this chapter presents a new view of the United States' experience, from advantageous viewing platforms provided by the European Economic Community (and the United Kingdom in particular), Canada, Australia, New Zealand, and Sweden.

The European Economic Community

The European Economic Community (EEC) was formed in 1957 by Belgium, France, Italy, Luxembourg, the Netherlands, and West Germany. Denmark, Ireland, and the United Kingdom acceded to the EEC in 1973, Greece in 1981, and Portugal and Spain in 1986, so there are currently twelve member states. The Treaty of Rome, the principal formative document of the EEC, contains an equal pay guarantee.[1] The official English version of Article 119 of the treaty reads as follows:

> Each Member State shall . . . ensure and subsequently maintain . . . the principle that men and women should receive equal pay for equal work.[2]

Until 1975, there was a great deal of uncertainty about the meaning and implementation of Article 119. In 1960, for example, the President of the Commission of the European Communities, the executive organ of the EEC, said that in his opinion the article did not encompass the notion of comparable worth, but merely required equal pay for the same work.[3] Similarly, in

1961, when all six member states reported that the principle of equal pay had been implemented, the EEC's Committee on Social Affairs and Public Health commented that the significant disparity between male and female wages in the states cast doubt on the accuracy of the governments' claims. The committee, though, was reluctant to reach any firm conclusions about compliance with Article 119 because it could not articulate the precise meaning of the equal pay guarantee, let alone decide whether it had been implemented.[4]

In 1975, the Council of Ministers of the European Communities, the principal legislative branch of the EEC, adopted a directive to clarify the meaning of Article 119.[5] The directive defined the equal pay guarantee of Article 119 so as to include comparable worth:

> The principle of equal pay for men and women outlined in Article 119 . . . means for the same work *or for work to which equal value is attributed,* the elimination of all discrimination on grounds of sex with regard to all aspects and conditions of remuneration.[6]

The directive also stated that:

> [W]here a job classification system is used for determining pay, it must be based on the same criteria for both men and women and so drawn up as to exclude any discrimination on grounds of sex.[7]

Thus, although the directive was vague on the precise meaning of equal value, it did indicate by inference that job evaluation systems were one method of establishing equal value. Finally, the directive required member states to enact laws to fully effectuate the "equal pay for work of equal value" principle.

All of the member states have now come into at least a shaky compliance with the directive, although seven did so only after infringement proceedings were initiated by the Commission of the European Communities.[8] This section will review only the experience of the United Kingdom.[9] Of the EEC member states, the United Kingdom's legal system is most similar to ours, it has had the longest experience with a comparable worth statute, and its process of compliance with the 1975 directive has been particularly dramatic.

The United Kingdom initially enacted a comparable worth statute in 1970, three years before it acceded to the EEC and became subject to Article 119 of the Treaty of Rome.[10] The effective date of the statute, however, was delayed until 1975 to give employers time to accommodate their practices to the new statutory obligations. The statute was entitled the Equal Pay Act 1970[11] and, although it was based in part on the United States Equal Pay Act of 1963,[12] it extended beyond the notion of equal pay for equal work and required equal pay for work of equal value.

The Equal Pay Act 1970 required equal pay for men and women in two circumstances. First, the statute required men and women to be paid equally if they were employed on "like work" in the same establishment. Like work was defined as work of "the same or a broadly similar nature" where any differences "are not of practical importance." However, even if men and women were performing like work, pay disparities were permissible if the employer could prove that the disparities were due to a "material difference" other than sex. Thus, if Freeda Peeples and a man were both employed by E.M. Ployer as nurses, the Equal Pay Act would require that they be paid equally unless the employer could demonstrate a material difference other than sex that would justify a pay disparity. This portion of the statute, though, would not require E.M. Ployer to pay nurses and janitors equally because they are not engaged in "like work." In this respect, the Equal Pay Act 1970 mirrors the United States' Equal Pay Act. The issues raised by the two statutes are identical: Are males and females doing like or equal work, or are there differences in the work that are of practical importance? If the work is like or equal, are there material differences other than sex that justify any pay disparity? Moreover, the two equal pay acts are of similar limited utility in rectifying the wage gap between men and women. To the extent the wage gap is present because women work in different and lower-paying jobs than men, it will not be affected by statutes that require equal pay for like or equal jobs.

The British act, however, extended beyond the American statute. The British statute also required equal pay where a woman was employed on work "rated as equivalent" with that of a man in the same employment. Section 1(5) of the act explained the "rated as equivalent" language:

> A woman is to be regarded as employed on work rated as equivalent with that of men if, but only if, her job and their job have been given an equal value, in terms of the demand made on a worker under various headings (for instance effort, skill, decision), on a study undertaken with a view to evaluating in those terms the jobs to be done by all or any of the employees in an undertaking or group of undertakings, or would have been given an equal value but for the evaluation being made on a system setting different values for men and women on the same demand under any heading.

Thus, if E.M. Ployer's nurses and janitors have been rated as equivalent by a job evaluation study, the Equal Pay Act 1970 required that they be paid equally. The Equal Pay Act 1970, then, contained a comparable worth guarantee. The structure of the act, however, limited the guarantee in a number of ways. First, comparable worth would only be recognized under the statute if the claim were based on a job evaluation study. Comparable worth claims were not cognizable under the statute if they were based on economic, sociological, or historical studies or indeed any type of study other than a job evaluation study. Second, only certain types of job evaluation studies could be used to prove that jobs were equivalent. Quantitative studies—studies using the factor comparison or point method—were cognizable under the act; qualitative studies—studies using the ranking or classification methods— were not.[13] Third, and most importantly, job evaluation studies could only be carried out in the United Kingdom with the agreement of the relevant parties, including the employer.[14] Thus, jobs could only be "rated as equivalent" based on a job evaluation study, but a job evaluation study could only be conducted if the employer agreed. It should not be surprising that few employers agreed to conduct job evaluation studies while this situation persisted and that, as a consequence, by 1979 the comparable worth provisions of the Equal Pay Act 1970 had become largely a dead letter.[15]

In 1979, the Commission of the European Communities reported on the progress of the member states in implementing the equal pay guarantee of Article 119, as defined by the 1975 directive.[16] The commission stated, as it had in the 1975 directive, that Article 119 required not only equal pay for equal work, but also equal pay for "work to which equal value is attributed." Moreover, the commission said that scientific job evaluation studies could not be the only method for establishing equal value. The commission concluded that, although substantial progress had been made, none of the member states had completely implemented Article 119's principle of equal pay. As a result, the commission announced its intention to commence infringement proceedings against several of the member states.

The infringement proceeding against the United Kingdom culminated in a decision by the European Court of Justice. In *Commission of the European Communities v. United Kingdom of Great Britain and Northern Ireland,* the European Court ruled that the United Kingdom's Equal Pay Act 1970 did not comply with Article 119 and the 1975 directive.[17] The court gave two principal reasons for its holding. First, job evaluations were merely one of several methods of determining equal value under the 1975 directive, but were the sole method under the British act; and second, since a job evaluation study could be introduced only with the employer's consent, the British act denied the right to equal pay for work of equal value to workers whose employers had not agreed to a study. The court flatly rejected the claim of the United Kingdom that the reliance on consensual job evaluation studies was necessary because the equal value criterion was too abstract to be applied by the courts. The court held that the 1975 directive required member states to grant jurisdiction to an authority to decide whether work has the same value as other work.

The Equal Pay Act 1970 was amended in response to the European Court of Justice decision.[18] The Equal Pay Act 1970 identified two situations where equal pay is required: (1) where a woman and a man perform "like" work and (2) where a job evaluation study ranks a woman's work and a man's work as equivalent. The Equal Pay Amendments added a third situation. Under the amendments, equal pay is also required "where a woman is employed on work which . . . is, in terms of demands made on her (for instance under such headings as effort, skill and decision), of equal value to that of a man in the same employment." As a result, if E.M. Ployer employs Freeda Peeples as a nurse and a man as a janitor, Freeda has a right to be paid the same as the man if their work is of equal value even though it is not like work and even if no job evaluation has been done.

The Equal Pay Amendments also provided a procedure for equal value cases. Freeda would commence her case by filing a claim with an Industrial Tribunal. An Industrial Tribunal is a type of administrative agency composed of a legally qualified chairperson and two lay representatives. The Industrial Tribunal would first examine Freeda's claim to determine if there were "reasonable grounds for determining that the work is of equal value." If there were no "reasonable grounds," the tribunal would dismiss the claim without further proceedings. Significantly, the Equal Pay Amendments provide that there are no reasonable grounds if Freeda's work was given a different (and presumably lower) value than the janitor's work on a job evaluation study. If Freeda's claim is not dismissed, the Industrial Tribunal will commission a report from a member of a panel of independent experts. The expert compares Freeda's job with that of the janitor and files a written report with the Industrial Tribunal. The Industrial Tribunal then holds a hearing in which the parties may cross-examine the expert. Each party may also call one expert witness to testify on its behalf. The Industrial Tribunal then renders a decision, which may be appealed to an Employment Appeals Tribunal, to the Court of Appeals, and eventually to the House of Lords.

The Equal Pay Amendments became effective on January 1, 1984. Although there are over 100 equal value cases currently in litigation, decisions in the first cases are only now beginning to be reported. In *Hayward v. Cammell Laird Shipbuilders Ltd.*, for example, a female shipyard cook claimed that she was employed on work of equal value to that of men employed as painters, insulators, and joiners.[19] An independent expert evaluated the jobs on the basis of five factors—physical demands, environmental demands, planning and decision making, skill and knowledge, and responsibility—and determined that the cook's work was of equal value to that of her male comparators. The Industrial Tribunal accepted the expert's report and ruled in favor of the cook.

The Equal Pay Amendments have not quelled the comparable worth debate in the United Kingdom. Many believe that the amendments are insufficient to bring the United Kingdom into compliance with Article 119, the 1975 directive, and the European Court of Justice decision. Indeed, in a highly unusual move, the House of Lords attached an amendment to the

Equal Pay Amendments that reads "that this House believes that [the Equal Pay Amendments] do not adequately reflect the 1982 decision of the European Court of Justice and . . . the EEC Equal Pay Directive of 1975." The problem is that the 1982 decision said that job evaluation studies were not to be the sole method for determining equal value, while the Equal Pay Amendments provide that the equal value procedure is to be terminated at an early stage if a job evaluation study ranked the male and female jobs in question differently. Thus, an employer need only commission a job evaluation study to effectively deny his employees the right to bring equal value claims.[20] While this does not have any direct effect on the Equal Pay Amendments, it may lead to another challenge to the United Kingdom's laws in the European Court.[21] Complaints have also come from those who believe that the Equal Pay Amendments have gone too far. Employer representatives have argued that the ripple effects of equal value pay awards are unknown but will, at the very least, be inflationary. For example, the award to the cook in the *Cammell Laird* case resulted in her earning more than her male coworkers and supervisor. It might be expected that considerable readjustment will need to be made in the next round of wage negotiations.

The United Kingdom's approach to comparable worth is interesting for Americans both procedurally and substantively. Procedurally, the contrast could hardly be more striking. The British have opted for an administrative procedure where class actions are not permitted and where the goal is quick, informal, and inexpensive settlement of disputes. In the United States, comparable worth cases are always class actions and are generally contested by two teams of lawyers over a period of years. Although it is far too early to make definitive judgments about the preferable approach, the contrasting approaches will be interesting and instructive to observe. Will the British procedure result in more cases being decided more quickly and, hence, in a rapidly developing body of law to guide employers and workers? Or will the perceived ripple effect of pay awards preclude quick and informal settlements and result in an increasing lawyerization of the process? Will the American procedure result in more carefully considered and, hence, more reliable precedent? Or will the expense of litigation deter so many litigants that important issues go unresolved?

Substantively, the British have opted for a relatively pure job comparison approach: a woman is entitled to the same pay as a man if the demands of her job are equal to the demands of his job. Although American jurisprudence seems to be headed in that direction, there is still some recognition that the underlying basis of comparable worth is discrimination and that discrimination may exist irrespective of the results of a job comparison. For example, if Freeda's nursing job is found to be less demanding than that of janitors, she is not entitled to equal pay under the British Equal Pay Amendments. But if discrimination is the basis of comparable worth, instead of mere job comparisons, Freeda may still be entitled to equal pay if she can prove by other means—say, by the use of sociological or economic studies—that nurses would have been paid more if the occupation were not female dominated. Thus, the British experience merits watching as an experiment with a relatively pure job comparison approach.

Canada

In Canada, the federal government and every province has equal pay legislation. In all but two of these jurisdictions, the legislation requires only equal pay for the same or similar work and, hence, does not encompass comparable worth.[22] The federal and Quebec statutes, however, require a form of comparable worth and merit closer scrutiny.

The federal law, the Canadian Human Rights Act, was enacted in 1977 and came into force in 1978. It applies to employees of the federal public service, of federal Crown corporations and agencies, and of federally regulated companies such as banks and the transportation and communications industries; approximately 11 percent of the Canadian work force is covered. Section 11(1) of the act requires equal wages for "male and female employees employed in the same establishment who are performing work of equal value." Equal value is to be assessed, according to Section 11(2) of the act, based on an evaluation of the skill, effort, responsibility, and working conditions of the work to be performed. Wage disparities between work of equal value are not illegal, however, if the disparities are based on factors approved by the Canadian Human Rights Commission. Some of the factors approved by the commission, such as formalized performance ratings and seniority, are fairly standard, but others, such as labor shortages or technological changes, are not. At least one commentator thinks that the strong provisions of the Canadian Human Rights Act have been undermined by the broad factors recognized by the commission to justify wage disparities between work of equal value.[23]

The Quebec Charter of Human Rights and Freedoms requires every employer "without discrimination, [to] grant equal salary or wages to the members of his personnel who perform equivalent work at the same place."[24] Although the term "equivalent work" could be interpreted to mean the same or similar work, it has been interpreted more broadly to cover work that, although different, has been rated as equivalent by a job evaluation system. In a case involving the Quebec North Shore Paper Company, for example, women employed as clerks and telephone operators were successful in obtaining pay raises under the act because their work had been rated by job evaluation as equivalent to that of men employed as land and wood measurers.[25]

The Canadian Human Rights Act and the Quebec Charter of Human Rights and Freedoms have similar enforcement procedures. In both, a complaint is initially filed with an enforcement commission. The commission investigates the complaint and attempts to negotiate a settlement. If settlement is not possible, the Quebec law is enforced directly in the courts, while under the Canadian law an administrative tribunal is appointed to hear evidence and to render a decision that can be enforced or challenged in federal court.

The Canadian comparable worth laws, like those in the United Kingdom, have been strongly influenced by international law. In 1951, the International Labour Organization adopted Convention No. 100, the "Convention Concerning Equal Remuneration for Men and Women Workers for Work of Equal Value."[26] This convention requires signatory nations to "ensure the application to all workers of the principle of equal remuneration for men and women workers for work of equal value." Canada ratified Convention No. 100 in 1972; the Quebec law was enacted in 1975, and the Canadian law in 1977. The Canadian law, in particular, closely follows the language of the Convention.

Also like the United Kingdom, the Quebec and Canadian laws use a job comparison, rather than a discrimination, approach to the comparable worth issue. That is, the focus of the legislation is on comparing jobs rather than on detecting discrimination. One consequence of this, illustrated by the Canadian experience, is that discrimination may continue unabated if an appropriate job comparison cannot be made. In *Public Service Alliance of Canada v. Treasury Board,* for example, female registered nursing assistants claimed that they were performing work of greater value than that of male orderlies, but that they were paid the same.[27] The enforcement commission dissuaded the nursing assistants from pursuing their claim under Section 11 of the Canadian Human Rights Act because the statute required only equal pay for equal value, it did not require greater pay for work of greater value. Thus, even though as a matter of discrimination there is no difference between paying women less for work of equal value and paying women the same for work of greater value, the job comparison approach resulted in prohibition of the former but not the latter.[28] Another consequence of the job comparison approach is that it may result in eradicating wage disparities that are not caused by discrimination. It must be assumed, for example, that a wage disparity between job classification A and job classification B is not caused by sex discrimination if both A and B have, and always have had, 95 percent male incumbents. But if the work of A and B is of equal value and a woman in the lower-paying classification brings an equal pay action, the language of both the Canadian and Quebec laws would support her claim. This matter is not of merely hypothetical concern. In *La Commission des Broits de la Personne du Quebec v. La Ferme de la Poulette Grise, Inc.,* three students who were employed for the summer claimed that the Quebec Charter of Human Rights was violated because they were paid less than permanent employees who were doing the same work.[29] Thus, the claim was of discrimination not between men and women, but between summer and permanent employees. The court avoided the issue for the time being by deciding the case on other grounds. The Canadian enforcement commission addresses this issue by requiring women bringing claims to be members of female-dominated occupations and comparator occupations to be male dominated.[30] This solution significantly narrows the gap between the job comparison and discrimination approaches; it is not, however, supported by the language of the statute which, on its face, imposes no such requirement.

Perhaps the most astounding aspect of the Canadian experience, at least to an American audience, is the low level of litigation under the statutes. In the first five-and-a-half years of the Canadian Human Rights Act, only two cases were commenced under Section 11 and only one was completed![31] The immediate domestic consequence of this low level of activity, of course, is the perception that the current laws are "an unsatisfactory response to the pervasiveness of systemic discrimination in Canadian workplaces" and a call by a federal commission for stronger laws.[32] The broader message, however, is that the enactment of laws may not lead to meaningful change. Change will occur only if the laws are enacted in circumstances that lead to compliance with the law. The circumstances required for compliance might take a number of forms; for example, they might include employers willing to voluntarily comply with a law, or the devotion of sufficient public resources to enforce the law and require employers to comply, or the presence of sufficiently powerful private groups (such as unions or women's rights groups) to enforce the law. The Canadian experience requires one to recognize that changing laws is only one way of dealing with the comparable worth issue and that merely changing laws, without close attention to the social milieu in which those laws are to operate, accomplishes little.

Australia

In Australia, the government plays a significant role in wage setting. Federal and state industrial tribunals issue awards that establish the pay of nearly 90 percent of all employees.[33] This section focuses on the activities of the federal wage-setting tribunal, the Australian Conciliation and Arbitration Commission, which is particularly influential because it establishes the pay of about 40 percent of the work force and because the state tribunals usually follow its lead.

There are three tiers to the federal wage-setting process.[34] In national wage cases, the first tier, senior members of the Arbitration Commission determine wages for all employees covered by federal awards based on macroeconomic indicators such as inflation, productivity, employment levels, and the balance of payments. Industry cases comprise the second tier of the process. In these cases, the Arbitration Commission (or the appropriate state tribunal) determines the wages of workers in particular industries based on the guidelines of the national wage case discussed above and the peculiar and relevant circumstances that affect the industry and workers in question. The third tier is beyond the ambit of the industrial tribunals. Depending on economic and political circumstances, unions may be able to negotiate "over-awards," that is, wages and/or benefits over those awarded by the industrial tribunal, for the employees of a particular company. The incidence of over-awards has varied over time, but it is generally the policy of the government and the Arbitration Commission to discourage them in the interest of a rational and centralized wage-setting process.

Examination of the sex discrimination laws in Australia reemphasizes the preeminence of this centralized process for determining wages. Four of the six Australian states have sex discrimination laws, but all but one of them exempt industrial awards and/or discriminatory wages and salaries from their prohibitions. The exemptions are designed to avoid conflict and confusion between industrial tribunals and anti-discrimination tribunals, but they also weaken the sex discrimination legislation and strengthen the centralized wage-setting process.[35] The federal government only recently passed its first sex discrimination law.[36] This tardiness was caused in part by a constitutional restriction that was removed by a High Court decision in 1983,[37] but also by the government's view that the Arbitration Commission and not the federal government was the proper body to resolve wage issues.[38] The federal sex discrimination law treads lightly on the prerogatives of the Arbitration Commission. The law exempts from the act "anything done . . . in direct compliance with . . . an order or award of [an industrial] tribunal."[39] Thus, a discriminatory wage rate contained in an award of the Arbitration Commission (or any other industrial tribunal) is not prohibited. The act does provide that industrial tribunals are not to issue discriminatory awards, but the effectiveness of this admonition is doubtful.[40] Arbitration Commission members hold their appointments until retirement and "have never interpreted their role as meekly responding to the wishes of the Federal Government."[41] Indeed, a leading Arbitration Judge once referred to himself and his colleagues as the "economic dictators of Australia."[42] Thus, the responsibility of dealing with the comparable worth issue is primarily that of the Arbitration Commission and the other industrial tribunals.

Some of the criteria used by the Arbitration Commission to determine wage levels seem to be quite conducive to comparable worth claims. Comparative wage justice, a traditional and pervasive criterion, requires that those doing work in one industry should be paid the same as those doing the same or similar work in other industries, regardless of productivity variations among industries.[43] The notion is one of equal pay for equal work, but it is broader than the concept in the United States because it operates across industries. Work value is another key wage-fixing concept. It requires the monetary worth of work to be assessed according to the nature of the work, the responsibilities involved, and the conditions under which it is performed. This, of course, sounds very similar to comparable worth claims in the United States except that, once again, it is broader because it cuts across industries and employers.

Despite these longstanding principles of wage determination, equal pay for women has had a tortured history in Australia. The first industrial tribunal case in which rates for women were discussed was the Fruit Packers case in 1912.[44] In that case, Mr. Justice Higgins held that the basic wage rate for women employed in female-dominated occupations should be less than the basic wage rate for men performing similar work because the women, unlike the men, did not generally support a family. Justice Higgins also ruled, however, that where women were employed in sexually mixed occupations, they should be paid the same as men because otherwise employers would tend to replace the men with lower-paid women. Later, in the Clothing Trades Award of 1919, Judge Higgins began the practice of fixing the female basic wage as a proportion of the male basic wage.[45]

For the next fifty years, substantial differences between male and female wages were a part of the structure of Australian wage setting. Until 1949, the women's wage rate was officially established at 54 percent of the male wage rate. In the 1949–1950 Basic Wage Inquiry, the Arbitration Commission increased the percentage to 75 percent, but it also rejected the claim for an equal wage rate for men and women.[46] Ironically, while the commission was restating its adherence to one part of the philosophy of Justice Higgins—"It was socially preferable to provide a higher wage for the male because of his social obligations to fiancee, wife and family"—the country was drifting away from another aspect of that philosophy.[47] Discrepancies between male and female wages were increasingly common in mixed occupations, despite the potential threat posed to male jobs. It was not until 1969 that the Arbitration Commission ruled that the principle of equal pay for work "of the same or a like nature and of equal value" should be applied in wage-setting cases.[48] But even then the ruling was quite limited because the commission ruled that the principle should not apply where the work was "essentially or usually performed by females." Thus, the ruling did not apply to female-dominated occupations, even though 82 percent of all women in the work force were engaged in occupations that were disproportionately female.[49] Finally, in 1972, the Arbitration Commission ruled that "the concept of 'equal pay for equal work' is too narrow in today's world and we think the time has come to enlarge the concept to 'equal pay for work of equal value.' This means that award rates for all work should be considered without regard to the sex of the employee."[50] Thus, since 1972, the comparable worth notion has been a policy of the centralized wage-setting process in Australia.

Despite the formal acceptance of comparable worth, there has been little actual progress in Australia. In 1969, when the first equal pay decision was rendered, the formal ratio of female to male wages was 75 percent. In January 1981, the actual ratio was 66.5 percent.[51] The formal changes in policy have been unable to overcome the tendency in Australia for wage differentials to remain unaltered once established. Some attribute this to the innate conservatism of industrial tribunals and to their fear of discontent if awards fail to preserve past relativities.[52] The tribunals are "patcher[s] of holes" and not "industrial architect[s]."[53] Others explain the failure by pointing to the absence of formal or informal job evaluation in Australia. Without job evaluation, the subtle, and often unconscious, undervaluation of women's work is likely to continue despite broad policy changes.[54]

Australia provides an interesting contrast to the United States. In America, one of the recurrent bogeymen of opponents of comparable worth is the prospect of centralized government boards setting wages. The Australian experience tends to undermine this criticism in two ways. First, Australia has existed for most of this century with government wage-setting boards and has, therefore, demonstrated that an industrialized country can operate quite nicely with a great deal of government involvement in wage setting. Second, Australia illustrates that government wage setting by itself, and indeed even government wage setting with an articulated comparable worth policy, may be insufficient to deal with the problem of unequal wages. Thus, if comparable worth in the United States leads to more government involvement in wage setting, it is likely that the economy could successfully adjust; but at the same time, the bogeyman of government wage boards is unlikely to materialize because, in Australia at least, they have proven to be an ineffective response to the problem.

New Zealand

New Zealand shares the wage-setting history and traditions of Australia. Since 1894, New Zealand has had a system of compulsory arbitration to resolve wage disputes and, until the 1970s, its treatment of equal pay issues mirrored that of Australia. But beginning in the early 1970s, New Zealand began to chart a separate course and this is particularly true on the comparable worth issue.

The Industrial Conciliation and Arbitration Act of 1894 established a wage-setting system consisting of voluntary negotiation, conciliation, and arbitration, supplemented by general wage orders. Unions voluntarily registered under the act and agreements between unions and employers were regulated by the state. Disputes were referred to a Council of Conciliation and, if they still could not be resolved, to a Court of Arbitration which had the power to issue binding awards.

As in Australia, this system's record on equal pay reflects the attitudes of the time of its origin. Differential wage rates were sanctioned as early as 1903, when the Court of Arbitration ordered male pieceworkers to be paid almost twice as much per hour as female pieceworkers. The legislature officially sanctioned differential rates in 1934 and 1945. The Industrial Conciliation and Arbitration Amendment Act of 1934 provided that the male basic wage rate should be sufficient to support a wife and three children in a fair and reasonable standard of comfort, while the female basic wage rate presumably need only be sufficient to support the individual worker. In 1945, the Minimum Wage Act provided for a female minimum of about 60 percent of the male minimum. In 1947, the Court of Arbitration continued its approval of wage differentials when it rejected an appeal to reduce the male-female differential to 90 percent. In rejecting the appeal, the court also introduced a jurisdictional issue that was to retard change for the next twenty-five years. The court said the equal pay issue was so fraught with social and economic consequences that it was more a matter for the legislature than the Court.[55]

Although small concessions to equalized wages were made by the court in 1949 and 1951, and although the legislature enacted statutes requiring equal pay for government employees in the 1960s, it was not until the 1970s that equal pay became a legal requirement in the private sector in New Zealand. Based on a report by a Commission of Inquiry into Equal Pay appointed by the government in 1970,[56] the Equal Pay Act of 1972 required "a rate of remuneration for work in which rate there is no element of differentiation between male employees and female employees based on the sex of the employees."[57] The act also provided criteria to apply to determine whether a difference exists between male and female remuneration. Where work is performed by both male and female employees, equal pay is required for work requiring the same or substantially similar skill, effort, and responsibility, and performed under the same or substantially similar conditions. Where work is performed exclusively or predominately by female employees, the women should be paid the same as male employees would be paid to perform the same, or substantially similar, work. Thus, where males and females perform the same work, women should be paid the same as men, and where only females perform a certain type of work, they should be paid the same as a notional or hypothetical man performing that same work. The Equal Pay Act provided that wage differentials were to be reduced in five approximately equal steps between October 1, 1973, and April 1, 1977. After April 1, 1977, all collective bargaining agreements and other documents setting wages were

Table 4–3
Female Earnings as a Percentage of Male Earnings in New Zealand, 1973 and 1977

	Female-Male Earnings Ratios	
	October 1973	*October 1977*
Overall		
Hourly earnings	71.3	78.5
Weekly earnings	68.3	76.0
Gross weekly earnings	61.7	70.8
Female-intensive industries		
Knitting mills	63.8	73.3
Laundries and laundry services	64.0	75.6
Data processing	57.6	63.8
Welfare institutions	71.5	87.5
Male-intensive industries		
Manufacture of fertilizers and pesticides	66.3	74.8
Manufacture of glass and glass products	60.3	80.3
Ocean and coastal water transport	56.3	67.8
Machinery and equipment rental and leasing	64.4	75.8

Source: Adapted from *Equal Pay Implementation in New Zealand* (Wellington: P. D. Hasselberg, 1979), 15–21.

to provide for equal pay. Thus, New Zealand opted for a legal approach to the comparable worth issue, despite its history of compulsory arbitration.

In 1979, New Zealand assessed its progress under the Equal Pay Act. A committee appointed by the Minister of Labour reported that substantial progress had been made in reducing the earnings disparity between men and women during the implementation period of the Act.[58] (See table 4–3.) The committee also examined the costs of equal pay in terms of inflation and unemployment. The committee estimated that equal pay efforts had increased the consumers' price index by approximately 3.25 percent between 1972 and 1977. The overall increase in the index for that period was 64.1 percent. On unemployment, the committee said that equal pay implementation was consistent with a significant increase in female employment. The committee noted increases in unemployment in some sections of the economy, but attributed them to general economic conditions rather than to equal pay efforts.

New Zealand, then, is a country where substantial progress has been made in a relatively short period of time to close the earnings gap between men and women. But the effort is both promising and disappointing for comparable worth advocates. It is promising because the progress was made with relatively minor inflation and unemployment repercussions. On the other hand, despite the progress, a substantial and persistent earnings gap remains, which underscores the resistance of the problem to purely legal solution.

Sweden

Sweden is fertile ground for comparative legal analysis because its approach to social problems often diverges considerably from that of the United States. The United States, for example, has used monetary and fiscal policy to attack unemployment and has attempted to promote healthy industrial competition through antitrust legislation and enforcement. Sweden, in contrast, has used state-owned enterprises that compete with private industry as a principal means of dealing with these same problems.[59] The Swedish approach to the comparable worth issue is also quite different. Instead of the legislation and litigation that epitomizes the American approach, Sweden has made great progress through extralegal channels, specifically through its system of centralized collective bargaining.

There is a longstanding tradition in Sweden that the government should not intervene in industrial relations, and especially not in wage negotiations. The government has never imposed wage rates or a wage freeze; minimum wage legislation has never even been proposed. This policy of nonintervention has also been observed with respect to the comparable worth issue. In 1952, the Minister of Social Affairs concluded that Sweden should not ratify the then-recent International Labour Organization Convention on Equal Remuneration[60] because ratification would mean "deviation from the principle that the parties on the labour market are entitled to agree upon wages through free negotiations without interference from the State."[61] The convention was ratified nearly a decade later, after substantial progress had been made through the collective bargaining process. The delay ensured that ratification would not require legislation to implement the equal pay principle and, as a result, the nonintervention principle was honored. More recently, the nonintervention principle appears to have survived the enactment of Sweden's first antidiscrimination statute. In 1979, the Act on Equal Opportunities for Women and Men at Work was passed.[62] The act prohibits sex discrimination in employment with general language, but the primary enforcer of the act—the Equality Ombudsman—is authorized to act only if the union involved explicitly refuses to take action and only if there is no interference with existing collective bargaining agreements. Moreover, the Equality Ombudsman is guided by statutory policy principles that emphasize voluntarism and cooperation.[63] Thus, although some state intervention is clearly contemplated, the act pays significant homage to the nonintervention principle and

Table 4–4
Female Earnings as a Percentage of Male Earnings in Selected Industrialized
Countries, 1976 and 1981[a]

	1976	1981	Change
Australia	79.0	80.4	1.4
Canada	62.1[b]	63.6	1.5
New Zealand	71.3	71.6	0.3
Sweden	86.9	90.1	3.2
United Kingdom	70.2	68.8	− 1.4
United States	60.2	59.2	− 1.0

Sources: Adapted from International Labour Office, *Women at Work*, no. 1 (Geneva: International Labour Office, 1983), 5; Statistics Canada, Social and Economic Studies Division, *Women in Canada A Statistical Report* (Ottawa: Minister of Supply & Services Canada, 1985), 61; U.S. Department of Labor, *Time of Change: 1983 Handbook on Women Workers* (Washington, D.C.: U.S. Government Printing Office, 1983), 82.
[a]Because of differences in methodologies and data bases, strict comparisons between countries should not be made on the basis of these statistics.
[b]1977

reflects the belief that private collective bargaining is Sweden's primary anti-discrimination tool.

Despite the principle of nonintervention, Sweden has been the most successful of the countries studied in narrowing the wage gap. In 1976, Sweden's wage gap was significantly less than that of the other countries studied. Thus, further progress should have been more difficult. Nevertheless, Sweden made the most progress in closing the gap in the next five years. (See table 4–4.)

The reasons for Sweden's success deserve a fuller treatment than can be provided here, but three aspects of Swedish labor relations provide a partial explanation. First, the trade union movement is much stronger in Sweden than it is in the United States. Over 90 percent of blue collar workers and about 70 percent of white collar workers are represented by unions affiliated with the two major national confederations, the Swedish Confederation of Trade Unions (LO) for blue collar workers and the Confederation of Salaried Employees (TCO) for white collar workers. Employers are highly organized, too; most firms are members of bargaining associations affiliated with the Swedish Employers' Confederation (SAF). Negotiations are conducted between the national employee and employer confederations to establish the terms and conditions of employment, including wages. Agreements between the national confederations are then adopted by individual unions and employers.[64] This centralized bargaining structure is more conducive to structural changes in wages policy than the decentralized structure in the United States. Second, the Swedish labor confederations (and particularly the LO) for a number of years have placed heavy reliance and have had some success on so-called "low-wage" claims—that is, claims on behalf of lower-paid workers.[65] Thus, some of the progress on male-female wage differentials in Sweden may be the result of generalized efforts on behalf of low-paid workers (who are disproportionately female), rather than efforts directed specifically at the effects of sex discrimination in the labor market. Third, wage equalization efforts in Sweden are aided by the widespread use of job evaluation plans. Formal job evaluation has been common for blue collar jobs since the 1950s and for white collar jobs since the 1960s.[66]

The progress in Sweden, however, is probably equally attributable to general attitudes on social welfare and the role of women. Predominant among these is the notion of wage solidarity. In Sweden, this means that the wage range should be as narrowly compressed as possible—that is, that workers, regardless of the nature of their jobs or their personal characteristics, should be paid the same wage. Thus, even if agreement cannot be reached on the reasons for the male-female wage disparity, the Swedish notion of wage solidarity provides a rationale for a narrowing of the disparity. In contrast, a basic assumption of wage setting in the United States is that differing jobs and personal qualifications justify wage differences. Thus, a prerequisite to progress on the male-female wage disparity is a demonstration that it is caused by sex discrimination rather than justifiable causes.

Sweden, then, has made substantial progress by pursuing a course dramatically different from that of the United States. In the United States, the comparable worth issue is primarily addressed through federal litigation and state legislation; in Sweden, the issue is primarily addressed through a centralized bargaining structure that emphasizes "low-wage" claims including those of female-dominated occupations.

Comments and Perspective

Comparative studies are only possible if countries address common concerns. Comparable worth, as this survey indicates, is a concern shared by many countries. The conditions that give rise to the issue—a male-female wage gap and occupational segregation—are present in the United States, in the Western industrialized countries surveyed here, and, indeed, in virtually every other country, including socialist and Third World countries.[67] At the same time, however, the United States is insulated from international forces that have played an important role in the approach of other countries to the issue. The United States is not a signatory to the International Labour Organization's Convention on Equal Remuneration nor, of course, has it signed the Treaty of Rome. Moreover, policymakers and commentators in the United States seem largely unaware of the approach of other countries to the issue.

This chapter's comparative survey has given us another perspective from which to judge the United States' experience. The variety of possible responses—from the use of government wage boards in Australia to reliance on the trade union movement in Sweden—indicates that the approach to the issue in the United States is not compelled by economic forces, but rather is primarily a product of history and habit. This unsurprising discovery is both promising and threatening. The promise is that the possible responses to the problem are broader than one with the blinders of history and habit firmly in place would think. The threat is that history and habit are not inconsiderable forces; they would likely be stubborn foes even if the blinders were removed.

The mixed results uncovered by the comparative survey pose another threat to efforts in the United States. Sweden seems to have had some success; the other countries, for the most part, have not. The ominous inference is that progress on the comparable worth issue depends as much on the social milieu as on the legal superstructure. But, of course, the social milieu is not as easily tinkered with as the legal superstructure.

Nevertheless, the overall impression left by the comparative survey is encouraging. The United States is not alone in battling an isolated virus, but instead is participating in a campaign against a widely shared epidemic. Although the mechanisms of a successful campaign remain mysterious, we know that progress is possible because it has been made elsewhere.

Afterword

The comparable worth issue is a topic of popular and heated debate. It should not be surprising that this is so. The issue involves work, money, sex, and the interrelationship between the three. That combination should be sufficient to enliven even the driest and most academic of political debates, let alone one like comparable worth that affects the everyday lives of millions of workers.

This book has participated in the debate in two ways. First, it has provided a theoretical structure through which the continuing developments can be viewed. Comparable worth is primarily an issue of discrimination. The crucial issue is not whether nurses are paid less than janitors for work requiring equal skill, effort, and responsibility, but whether nursing as an occupation is paid less than it would be if it were not female dominated. The former is relevant because it may help us determine the latter, but the latter is the issue to be addressed. Second, the book has participated in the comparable worth debate by presenting information and alternatives. The efforts of economists and lawyers and the experiences of Minnesota and Sweden should be useful in deciding where Local School District No. 1 should stand on the issue.

Nevertheless, books on topical subjects like comparable worth have the habit of becoming untopical fairly quickly. Even John Keats, who was quite good on enduring subjects ("A thing of beauty is a joy for ever"), would undoubtedly have been long forgotten if he had written only on more topical subjects ("[Woman] is like a milk-white lamb that bleats / For man's protection"). The goal of this book, then, is not to avoid its certain and nearby fate of aged quaintness, but merely to be of some use and assistance during its life of but a day.

Notes

Chapter 1. The Economics of Comparable Worth

1. U.S. Department of Labor, Women's Bureau, *Time of Change: 1983 Handbook on Women Workers* (Washington, D.C.: U.S. Government Printing Office, 1983), 81–82.

2. U.S. Commission on Civil Rights, *Comparable Worth: Issue for the 80's,* vol. 1 (Washington, D.C.: U.S. Government Printing Office, 1984), 8–10.

3. James P. Smith and Michael P. Ward, *Women's Wages and Work in the Twentieth Century* (Santa Monica, Calif.: The Rand Corp., 1984), 73–77.

4. Gary Becker, *Economics of Discrimination,* 2nd ed. (Chicago: The University of Chicago Press, 1971), 39–40.

5. Burton G. Malkiel and Judith A. Malkiel, "Male-Female Pay Differentials in Professional Employment," *American Economic Review* 63 (Sept. 1973):697–99.

6. For general discussions of this theory, see Gary S. Becker, *Human Capital* (New York: Columbia University Press, 1964); Gary S. Becker, "Investment in Human Capital: A Theoretical Analysis," *Journal of Political Economy* 70 (Oct. 1962):9–49.

7. In neoclassical economics, several conditions must be met for there to be perfect competition: large numbers of buyers and sellers so that the actions of individual buyers and sellers will not have a significant effect on prices and outputs; free entry into the market; homogeneous products; perfect knowledge; and frictionless mobility. See Alfred W. Stonier and Douglas C. Hague, *A Textbook of Economic Theory,* 5th ed. (London: Longman, 1980), 142–45; Joan Robinson, "What is Perfect Competition?" *The Quarterly Journal of Economics* (Nov. 1934):104–20.

8. The example is adapted from Donald J. Treiman and Heidi I. Hartmann, *Women, Work, and Wages: Equal Pay for Jobs of Equal Value* (Washington, D.C.: National Academy Press, 1981), 42–43.

9. Lester Thurow, *Generating Inequality* (New York: Basic Books, 1975), 160–62; Kenneth Arrow, "The Theory of Discrimination," in *Discrimination in Labor Markets,* ed. Orley Ashenfelter and Albert Rees (Princeton, N.J.: Princeton University Press, 1973), 10; Kenneth Arrow, "Models of Job Discrimination," in *Racial Discrimination in Economic Life,* ed. Anthony H. Pascal (Lexington, Mass.: D.C. Heath, 1972), 90.

10. See generally Treiman and Hartmann, *Women, Work, and Wages,* 18; Henry

Phelps Brown, *The Inequality of Pay* (Oxford: Oxford University Press, 1977); Michael J. Piore, ed., *Unemployment and Inflation* (White Plains, N.Y.: M.E. Sharpe, 1979).

11. See, for example, Treiman and Hartmann, *Women, Work, and Wages,* 18. But see Cheryl L. Maranto and Robert C. Rodgers, "Does Work Experience Increase Productivity? A Test of the On-the-Job Training Hypothesis," *Journal of Human Resources* 19 (summer 1984):341–57; Stanley A. Horowitz and Allan Sherman, "A Direct Measure of the Relationship between Human Capital and Productivity," *Journal of Human Resources* 15 (winter 1980):67–76.

12. For technical criticisms of the forward regression technique that is used in most of the studies, see Carole A. Green and Marianne A. Ferber, "Employment Discrimination: An Empirical Test of Forward Versus Reverse Regression," *Journal of Human Resources* 19 (fall 1984):557–69; Arthur S. Goldberger, "Reverse Regression and Salary Discrimination," *Journal of Human Resources* 19 (summer 1984):293–318.

13. See generally David W. Barnes, *Statistics as Proof* (Boston: Little, Brown, 1983), 293–395.

14. For a discussion of other limitations of the multiple regression technique, see Carl C. Hoffman and Dana Quade, "Regression and Discrimination," *Sociological Methods & Research* 11 (May 1983):407–42.

15. Cynthia B. Lloyd and Beth T. Neimi, *The Economics of Sex Differentials* (New York: Columbia University Press, 1979), 205; Jacob Mincer and Solomon Polachek, "Family Investments in Human Capital: Earnings of Women," *Journal of Political Economy* 82 (March/April 1974):S103–S104; Isabel V. Sawhill, "The Economics of Discrimination Against Women: Some New Findings," *Journal of Human Resources* 8 (summer 1973):384, 391–94.

16. U.S. Bureau of the Census, *1980 Census of Population, Subject Reports, Earnings by Occupation and Education* (Washington, D.C.: U.S. Government Printing Office, 1984), 1–252.

17. See Treiman and Hartmann, *Women, Work, and Wages,* 39–40.

18. For a more complete analysis of high- and low-paying occupations, see Nancy F. Rytina, "Earnings of Men and Women: A Look at Specific Occupations," *Monthly Labor Review* 105 (April 1982):25–31.

19. Occupation and/or occupational characteristics should not be included as variables in studies that adhere to pure human capital theory. If there were perfect mobility between occupations and industries, and people with full information were seeking the highest returns on their human capital investments, returns across occupations and industries should equalize. See Treiman and Hartmann, *Women, Work, and Wages,* 22.

20. See also, the Roos and Sanborn studies cited in table 1–6.

21. Victor R. Fuchs, "Differences in Hourly Earnings Between Men and Women," *Monthly Labor Review* 94 (May 1971):14. See also Treiman and Hartmann, *Women, Work, and Wages,* 33, n. 19.

22. David M. Gordon, "Economic Dimensions of Occupational Segregation—Comment II," in *Women and the Workplace,* ed. Martha Blaxall and Barbara Reagan (Chicago: University of Chicago Press, 1976), 240. See also Victor R. Fuchs, "Differ-

ences in Hourly Earnings Between Men and Women," *Monthly Labor Review* 94 (May 1971):14.

23. See Gary Becker, "A Theory of the Allocation of Time," *The Economic Journal* 80 (Sept. 1965):493–517; Jacob Mincer and Solomon Polachek, "Family Investments in Human Capital: Earnings of Women," *Journal of Political Economy* 82 (March/April 1974):S76–S108. See generally Francine D. Blau and Carol L. Jusenius, "Economists' Approaches to Sex Segregation in the Labor Market: An Appraisal," in *Women and the Workplace,* ed. Martha Blaxall and Barbara Reagan (Chicago: University of Chicago Press, 1976), 185–88.

24. See Treiman and Hartmann, *Women, Work, and Wages,* 53.

25. See generally Daniel W. Boothby, *The Determinants of Earnings and Occupation for Young Women* (New York: Garland, 1984).

26. For general descriptions of the internal labor market model, see Treiman and Hartmann, *Women, Work, and Wages,* 45–47; Blau and Jusenius, "Economists' Approaches," 190–99.

27. Under the neoclassical human capital approach, this would be likely to result in pay differences: employers would pay women less because of the increased risk associated with hiring them. The internal labor market model postulates a more rigid set of wage relationships and promotional opportunities, defined primarily in terms of job category. If pay differentials cannot be used to account for these group-based differences, some type of hiring discrimination is likely.

28. Bureau of National Affairs, *Pay Equity and Comparable Worth* (Washington, D.C.: Bureau of National Affairs, 1984), 72.

29. Donald J. Treiman, Heidi I. Hartmann, and Patricia A. Roos, "Assessing Pay Discrimination Using National Data" in *Comparable Worth and Wage Discrimination,* ed. Helen Remick (Philadelphia: Temple University Press, 1984), 137–154.

30. Title VII of the Civil Rights Act of 1964 is the statute that is commonly used in comparable worth cases. It covers only employers that employ fifteen or more employees. 42 U.S.C. sec. 2000e(b)(1982).

31. Chapter 2 discusses comparable worth litigation and its costs.

32. Treiman, Hartmann, and Roos, "Assessing Pay Discrimination," 151.

33. See generally Michael Evan Gold, *A Dialogue on Comparable Worth* (Ithaca, N.Y.: ILR Press, 1983), 54–64; E. Robert Livernash, ed., *Comparable Worth: Issues and Alternatives* (Washington, D.C.: Equal Employment Advisory Council, 1980), 102–106.

34. Bureau of National Affairs, *Pay Equity and Comparable Worth* (Washington, D.C.: Bureau of National Affairs, 1984), 72.

35. Brian Chiplin and Peter J. Sloane, *Tackling Discrimination at the Workplace* (Cambridge: Cambridge University Press, 1982), 122.

Chapter 2. Comparable Worth Litigation

1. *AFSCME v. State of Washington,* 578 F. Supp. 846 (W.D. Wash. 1983). The decision was later reversed on appeal. *AFSCME v. State of Washington,* 770 F.2d 1401 (9th Cir. 1985).

2. See *International Union of Electrical Workers v. Westinghouse Electric Corp.*, 631 F.2d 1094 (3d Cir. 1980), *cert. denied*, 449 U.S. 1009 (1980); *Briggs v. City of Madison*, 536 F.Supp. 435 (W.D. Wis. 1982).

3. See *Spaulding v. University of Washington*, 740 F.2d 686 (9th Cir.), *cert. denied*, 105 S.Ct. 511 (1984); *Christensen v. Iowa*, 563 F.2d 353 (8th Cir. 1977).

4. 29 U.S.C. sec. 206(d)(1982). In every state except Alabama, Louisiana, and Mississippi, state laws also prohibit employment discrimination. Most of the state laws are modeled on either the Equal Pay Act of 1963 or Title VII of the Civil Rights Act of 1964, 42 U.S.C. secs. 2000e to 2000e-17 (1982). Most of what is said in this chapter is directly applicable to litigation under those state laws. State employment discrimination laws that deal more specifically with the comparable worth issue will be discussed in chapter 3.

5. 107 *Cong. Rec.* 17,574–17,576 (1961); *H.R. Rep.* no. 1714 (1962).

6. 108 *Cong. Rec.* 14,767–14,771 (1962).

7. 29 U.S.C. sec. 206(d) (1982).

8. 109 *Cong. Rec.* 9197 (1963).

9. Freeda Peeples will be used a number of times in this book as an example. She and E.M. Ployer, who will be introduced later, are purely hypothetical and any resemblance to actual persons is entirely coincidental.

10. *H.R. Rep.* no. 914 (1964).

11. 110 *Cong. Rec.* 2577, 2584 (1964).

12. 42 U.S.C. secs. 2000e to 2000e-17 (1982).

13. 42 U.S.C. sec. 2000e-2(a)(1) (1982).

14. An intent to discriminate may be relevant in some circumstances. See *Albemarle Paper Co. v. Moody*, 422 U.S. 405, 425 (1975). For a more detailed discussion of the disparate impact model of discrimination, see Steven L. Willborn, "The Disparate Impact Model of Discrimination: Theory and Limits," *American University Law Review* 34, no. 3(1985):799–837.

15. See *EEOC v. Federal Reserve Bank*, 698 F.2d 633, 638–39 (4th Cir. 1983); *Peques v. Mississippi State Employment Service*, 699 F.2d 760, 765 (5th Cir. 1983); *Harris v. Ford Motor Co.*, 26 E.P.D. para. 31,906 (8th Cir. 1981).

16. For a forceful argument that the judicial role should be limited to this type of situation, see John Hart Ely, *Democracy and Distrust: A Theory of Judicial Review* (Cambridge, Mass.: Harvard University Press, 1980), 73–104.

17. Plaintiffs' only major victory in the federal courts has recently been overturned on appeal. *AFSCME v. State of Washington*, 578 F. Supp. 846 (W.D. Wash. 1983), *rev'd*, 770 F.2d 1401 (9th Cir. 1985).

18. For an analysis of the litigiousness of Americans, see Marc Galanter, "Reading the Landscape of Disputes: What We Know and Don't Know (and Think We Know) About Our Allegedly Contentious and Litigious Society," *UCLA Law Review* 31 (Oct. 1983):4–71.

Chapter 3. Comparable Worth Legislation

1. This survey was conducted in June, 1985.

2. The following twenty-six states have established bodies to study comparable

worth issues with respect to public employees: California, Connecticut, Delaware, Hawaii, Indiana, Iowa, Maryland, Massachusetts, Michigan, Minnesota, Montana, Nevada, New Jersey, New Mexico, New York, North Carolina, Ohio, Oregon, Rhode Island, South Dakota, Vermont, Virginia, Washington, West Virginia, Wisconsin, and Wyoming. Four other states—Alaska, Arizona, Louisiana, and Maine—have established bodies to review the state's general compensation scheme, and those bodies may also consider comparable worth issues as part of their deliberations.

3. The task forces in Massachusetts and New York, in contrast to those in Alaska, Arizona, Louisiana, and Maine (see the previous footnote), have been specifically directed to examine the comparable worth issue.

4. The states rejecting bills to establish task forces are Colorado, Florida, Illinois, Kansas, Maine, Missouri, Nebraska, North Dakota, Pennsylvania, and Texas.

5. The following states have not yet taken any action on the issue: Alabama, Arkansas, Georgia, Idaho, Kentucky, Mississippi, New Hampshire, Oklahoma, South Carolina, Tennessee, and Utah.

6. Hawaii suspended the operations of its task force because of pending litigation, and North Carolina suspended the operations of its task force after it became dissatisfied with the direction of the study.

7. 578 F. Supp. 846 (W.D. Wash. 1983), rev'd, 770 F.2d 1401 (9th Cir. 1985).

8. The following states have authorized or completed professional job evaluations: Connecticut, Delaware, Iowa, Maryland, Minnesota, North Carolina, South Dakota, Washington, West Virginia, and Wyoming. North Carolina hired a consultant to conduct the job evaluation, but killed the project before it was completed.

9. For good general discussions of job evaluation methodology, see Richard W. Beatty and James R. Beatty, "Some Problems with Contemporary Job Evaluation Systems" in *Comparable Worth and Wage Discrimination,* ed. Helen Remick (Philadelphia: Temple University Press, 1984), 59–78; Donald J. Treiman, *Job Evaluation: An Analytic Review* (Washington, D.C.: National Academy of Sciences, 1979); Dov Elizur, *Job Evaluation: A Systematic Approach* (Westmead, England: Gower, 1980).

10. Bureau of National Affairs, *Job Evaluation Policies and Procedures* (Washington, D.C.: Bureau of National Affairs, 1976), 2, 4; Mustafa T. Akalin, *Office Job Evaluation* (Des Plaines, Ill.: Industrial Management Society, 1970), 62–63, 70–75, 81.

11. See International Labour Organisation, *Job Evaluation* (Geneva: International Labour Office, 1960), 22; Elizabeth Lanham, *Job Evaluation* (New York: McGraw-Hill, 1955), 52.

12. International Labor Organisation, *Job Evaluation,* 23.

13. This example is adapted from Treiman, *Job Evaluation: An Analytic Review,* 3.

14. See, Akalin, *Office Job Evaluation,* 72; Bryan Livy, *Job Evaluation: A Critical Review* (New York: John Wiley, 1975), 91.

15. See Donald J. Treiman and Heidi I. Hartmann, *Women, Work, and Wages: Equal Pay for Jobs of Equal Value* (Washington, D.C.: National Academy Press, 1981), 72; Treiman, *Job Evaluation: An Analytic Review,* 31.

16. The point method is used to discuss these concerns because it is the most popular of the job evaluation methods. Most of the concerns discussed, however, are equally applicable to the other methods of job evaluation.

17. The validity issue will be discussed later in this chapter.

18. Donald J. Treiman, "Effect of Choice of Factors and Factor Weights in Job Evaluation," in *Comparable Worth and Wage Discrimination,* ed. Helen Remick (Philadelphia: Temple University Press, 1984), 88; Akalin, *Office Job Evaluation,* 43–50.

19. See Treiman, *Job Evaluation: An Analytic Review,* 34–39, 40–43; Donald P. Schwab, "Job Evaluation and Pay Setting: Concepts and Practices," in *Comparable Worth: Issues and Alternatives,* ed. E. Robert Livernash (Washington, D.C.: Equal Employment Advisory Council, 1980), 59–61; Akalin, *Office Job Evaluation,* 51–55, and the studies cited therein.

20. Reliability is a necessary but not a sufficient condition for validity. See generally, Julian C. Stanley and Kenneth D. Hopkins, *Educational and Psychological Measurement and Evaluation* (Englewood Cliffs, N.J.: Prentice-Hall, 1972), 114–17. That is, if the point method is reliable it may be valid, but if it is not reliable it cannot be valid.

21. Richard W. Beatty and James R. Beatty, "Job Evaluation and Discrimination: Legal, Economic, and Measurement Perspectives on Comparable Worth and Women's Pay" in *Women in the Work Force,* ed. H. John Bernardin (New York: Praeger, 1982), 226; Schwab, "Job Evaluation and Pay Setting," 58–59; Equal Employment Advisory Council, *Comparable Worth: A Symposium on the Issues and Alternatives* (Washington, D.C.: Equal Employment Advisory Council, 1981), 96.

22. Treiman, *Job Evaluation: An Analytic Review,* 1.

23. Elizur, *Job Evaluation: A Systematic Approach,* 5.

24. Helen Remick, "Major Issues in *a priori* Applications," in *Comparable Worth and Wage Discrimination,* ed. Helen Remick (Philadelphia: Temple University Press, 1984), 113.

25. Female workers are not rated less favorably than male workers when the evaluators are provided with independent grounds for believing the female workers are competent. See, for example, M.M. Clifford and W.R. Looft, "Academic Employment Interviews: Effect of Sex and Race," *Educational Research* 22 (1971):6–8; G.I. Pheterson, S.B. Kiesler, and P.A. Goldberg, "Evaluation of the Performance of Women as a Function of Their Sex, Achievement, and Personal History," *Journal of Personality and Social Psychology* 19 (1971):114–18; Elaine Walster, T. Anne Cleary, and Margaret M. Clifford, "Research Note: The Effect of Race and Sex on College Admission," *Sociology of Education* 41 (spring 1970):237–44.

26. Benson Rosen and Thomas H. Jerdee, "Effects of Applicant's Sex and Difficulty of Job on Evaluations of Candidates for Managerial Positions," *Journal of Applied Psychology* 59 (Aug. 1974):511–12; Benson Rosen and Thomas H. Jerdee, "Sex Stereotyping in the Executive Suite," *Harvard Business Review* 52 (March-April 1974):45–58; Benson Rosen and Thomas H. Jerdee, "Influence of Sex Role Stereotypes on Personnel Decisions," *Journal of Applied Psychology* 59 (Feb. 1974): 9–14; L.S. Fidell, "Empirical Verification of Sex Discrimination in Hiring Practices," *American Psychologist 25 (1970):1094–98.*

27. Mary Witt and Patricia K. Naherny, *Women's Work: Up From .878* (Madison, Wis.: University of Wisconsin-Extension, 1975).

28. For a discussion of the effect of this type of error on the validity of a job evaluation, see Donald P. Schwab and Dean W. Wichern, "Systematic Bias in Job Evaluation and Market Wages: Implications for the Comparable Worth Debate," *Journal of Applied Psychology* 68 (Feb. 1983):60–69.

29. See chapter 2.

30. See chapter 1.

31. For a general discussion of these studies, see Ruth G. Blumrosen, "Wage Discrimination, Job Segregation, and Title VII of the Civil Rights Act of 1964," *University of Michigan Journal of Law Reform* 12 (spring 1979):415–21.

32. Minn. Stat. sec. 43A(3)(1982).

33. Alabama, Louisiana, and Mississippi do not have equal pay or fair employment practices laws. Texas does not have a fair employment practices law and has an equal pay law that applies only to public sector employees. Tex. Stat. Ann. tit. 117, art. 6825 (Vernon 1960).

34. 42 U.S.C. secs. 2000e to 2000e-17 (1982).

35. 29 U.S.C. sec. 206(d) (1982).

36. See generally, Virginia Dean, Patti Roberts, and Carroll Boone, "Comparable Worth Under Various Federal and State Laws," in *Comparable Worth and Wage Discrimination,* ed. Helen Remick (Philadelphia: Temple University Press, 1984), 238–66.

37. In 1955, Pennsylvania enacted a law that required equal pay "for work under comparable conditions on jobs the performance of which requires comparable skills." Pa. Stat. Ann. tit. 43, sec. 336.3 (Purdon 1964). In 1968, Pennsylvania repealed that language and replaced it with language identical to that of the federal Equal Pay Act. Pa. Stat. Ann. tit. 43, sec. 336.3 (Purdon Supp. 1984).

38. For a more detailed discussion of comparable worth litigation under federal law, see chapter 2.

39. Prima facie, in this context, merely means that the plaintiff has presented proof sufficient to establish a violation of Title VII. If no other evidence were presented, the plaintiff would prevail.

40. See, *International Union of Electrical Workers v. Westinghouse Electric Corp.,* 631 F.2d 1094 (3d Cir. 1980), *cert. denied,* 452 U.S. 967 (1981); *AFSCME v. State of Washington,* 578 F. Supp. 846 (W.D. Wash. 1983), *rev'd,* 770 F.2d 1401 (9th Cir. 1985); *Briggs v. City of Madison,* 536 F. Supp. 435 (W.D. Wis. 1982).

41. See, *Christensen v. Iowa,* 563 F.2d 353 (8th Cir. 1977); *Spaulding v. University of Washington,* 740 F.2d 686 (9th Cir. 1984); *Lemons v. City and County of Denver,* 620 F.2d 228 (10th Cir.), *cert. denied,* 449 U.S. 888 (1980); *American Nurses Ass'n v. State of Illinois,* 37 FEP Cases 705 (N.D. Ill. 1985); *Francoeur v. Corroon & Black Co.,* 552 F. Supp. 403 (S.D.N.Y. 1982); *Gerlach v. Michigan Bell Telephone Co.,* 501 F. Supp. 1300 (E.D. Mich. 1980).

42. See chapter 2.

43. A greater showing may be required in Oklahoma. In contrast to the other state laws, the equal pay law in Oklahoma contains an intent element. An employer violates the Oklahoma law only if he "willfully" pays wages to women at a rate less than the rate paid to men for comparable work. Okla. Stat. Ann. tit. 40, sec. 198.1 (Supp. 1984–85). A plaintiff may have to make a greater showing to establish the intent element of a prima facie case.

44. The Alaska law is modeled after Title VII and, hence, allocates the burdens in the same way as Title VII. The other laws are all modeled after the Equal Pay Act of 1963 and, hence, adopt its allocation of burdens. See Michael J. Zimmer, Charles A. Sullivan, and Richard F. Richards, *Cases and Materials on Employment Discrimination* (Boston: Little, Brown, 1982), 575–76.

45. See, Charles A. Sullivan, Michael J. Zimmer, and Richard F. Richards, *Federal Statutory Law of Employment Discrimination* (Indianapolis: The Michie Co., 1980), 622–25.

46. General Accounting Office, *Options for Conducting a Pay Equity Study of Federal Pay and Classification Systems* (Washington, D.C.: U.S. Government Printing Office, 1985).

47. "Comparable-Worth Plans Make Few Inroads in the Private Sector, " *The Wall Street Journal,* April 16, 1985 (Midwest edition).

Chapter 4. Comparable Worth in Other Countries

1. Office for Official Publications of the European Communites, *Treaties Establishing the European Communities* (Luxembourg: Office for the Official Publications of the European Communities, 1973), 205–575. The treaty can also be found at "Treaty Establishing the European Economic Community," Nov. 23–Dec. 13, 1957, 298 *U.N.T.S.* 11. For a general discussion of the structure, rules, and practices of the EEC, see Sir Barnett Cocks, *The European Parliament* (London: Her Majesty's Stationery Office, 1973).

2. Office for Official Publications, *Treaties,* 312. A slightly different version appears at 298 *U.N.T.S.* at 62.

3. Excerpt from letter of Walter Hallstein, cited in Commission Sociale, "Rapport intérimaire sur l'égalisation des salaires masculins et féminins," *Assemblée Parlementaire Européenne, Documents de Seance,* no. 68 (1961):3.

4. Ibid., 11. See also Remarks of M. Motte, *Assemblée Parlementaire Européenne, Débats,* no. 46 (Oct. 20, 1961):258–60.

5. "Council Directive of 10 February 1975 on the approximation of the laws of the Member States relating to the application of the principle of equal pay for men and women," *Official Journal of the European Communities* 18 (no. L 45 1975):19–20. A directive is a form of EEC legislation that is binding on member states, but which allows the states to choose the form and method of implementation.

6. Ibid., 19 (emphasis added).

7. Ibid.

8. The infringement proceedings were against Belgium, Denmark, France, the Federal Republic of Germany, Luxembourg, the Netherlands, and the United Kingdom. C.E. Landau, "Recent Legislation and Case Law in the EEC on Sex Equality in Employment," *International Labour Review* 123 (Jan.-Feb. 1984):55, and n. 3.

9. For a brief review of the compliance activities of the other EEC member states, except for Portugal and Spain who have just recently acceded, see Janice R. Bellace, "A Foreign Perspective," in *Comparable Worth: Issues and Alternatives,* ed. E. Robert Livernash (Washington, D.C.: Equal Employment Advisory Council, 1980), 137–72; Commission of the European Communities, *Community Law and Women* (Brussels: Commission of the European Communities, 1983), 6–30.

10. Statutes enacted by the British Parliament generally apply only in Great Britain. They can, however, be extended to Northern Ireland. The Equal Pay Act 1970 and Sex Discrimination Act 1975 have, with limited modifications, been extended to

Northern Ireland. As a result, this chapter will refer to the United Kingdom, even though more exact phraseology would be technically appropriate.

11. The Equal Pay Act 1970, ch. 41, as amended.

12. 29 U.S.C. sec. 206(d) (1982). For a discussion of the Equal Pay Act of 1963, see chapter 2.

13. For a discussion of the different methods of job evaluation, see chapter 3.

14. *O'Brien v. Sim-Chem Limited,* [1980] I.R.L.R. 373, 374 (House of Lords).

15. Linda Clarke, "Proposed Amendments to the Equal Pay Act 1970–I," *New Law Journal* 133 (Oct. 1983):936.

16. Commission of the European Communities, *Report of the Commission to the Council on the Application as at 12 February 1978 of the Principle of Equal Pay for Men and Women,* COM (78)711 (Brussels: Commission of the European Communities, 1979).

17. [1982] I.R.L.R. 333.

18. Equal Pay (Amendment) Regulations 1983.

19. [1984] I.R.L.R. 463 (Industrial Tribunal).

20. Linda Clarke, "Proposed Amendments to the Equal Pay Act 1970–II," *New Law Journal* 133 (Dec. 1983):1130.

21. Linda Clarke, "Equal Pay for Work of Equal Value," *New Law Journal* 134 (Feb. 1984):177.

22. For a general review of Canadian discrimination laws, see Walter Surma Tarnopolsky, *Discrimination and the Law in Canada* (Toronto: Richard De Boo, 1982).

23. Shirley G.E. Carr, "Sex-Based Discrimination in Employment: Problems and Progress in Canada," *International Labour Review* 122 (Nov.-Dec. 1983):765.

24. Section 19, R.S.Q. 1977, c. C-12, as amended.

25. Tarnopolsky, *Discrimination and the Law in Canada,* 421.

26. International Labour Organisation, *International Labour Conventions and Recommendations 1919–1981* (Geneva: International Labour Office, 1982), 42–43.

27. The case was settled, so there is no case citation, but it is discussed in Rita Cadieux, "Canada's Equal Pay for Work of Equal Value Law," in *Comparable Worth and Wage Discrimination,* ed. Helen Remick (Philadelphia: Temple University Press, 1984), 184–86.

28. In fairness to the enforcement commission, it should be mentioned that some relief was found for the complainants under other sections of the Canadian Human Rights Act. Ibid.

29. 3 *Canadian Human Rights Reporter* para. 6235–6249 (1982).

30. Cadieux, "Canada's Equal Pay," 176–77.

31. Ibid., 186.

32. Report of the Commission on Equality in Employment, reported in 5 *Canadian Human Rights Reporter* ND/20. See also Carr, "Sex-Based Discrimination," 769.

33. Department of Industrial Relations, *Australian Industrial Relations Systems* (Canberra: Australian Government Publishing Services, 1980), 2.

34. See generally, Braham Dabscheck and John Niland, "Recent Trends in Collective Bargaining in Australia," *International Labour Review* 123 (Sept.-Oct. 1984):634–35.

35. See generally, Chris Ronalds, *Anti-Discrimination Legislation in Australia* (Sydney: Butterworth, 1979), 87–89.

36. Sex Discrimination Act 1984, No. 4 of 1984, assented to March 21, 1984, in force August 1, 1984.

37. *Commonwealth v. Tasmania,* 46 Australian Law Reports 625 (1983). See Dabscheck, "Recent Trends, " 634.

38. John Nieuwenhuysen and John Hicks, "Equal Pay for Women in Australia and New Zealand," in *Equal Pay for Women,* ed. Barrie O. Pettman (Bradford, England: MCB Books, 1975), 79–80.

39. Section 40, Sex Discrimination Act 1984.

40. Section 109, Sex Discrimination Act 1984.

41. Dabscheck, "Recent Trends," 632.

42. M. Perlman, *Judges in Industry: A Study of Labour Arbitration in Australia* (Melbourne: Melbourne University Press, 1954), 32.

43. John Niland, *Collective Bargaining and Compulsory Arbitration in Australia* (Kensington, Australia: New South Wales University Press, 1978), 61.

44. 6 Commonwealth Arbitration Reports 61 (1912).

45. 13 Commonwealth Arbitration Reports 647, 691–95 (1919).

46. 68 Commonwealth Arbitration Reports 698, 815–19 (1949).

47. Ibid., 816.

48. *Equal Pay Cases,* 127 Commonwealth Arbitration Reports 1142 (1969).

49. See *National Wage and Equal Pay Cases 1972,* 147 Commonwealth Arbitration Reports 172, 177 (1972). See also, Margaret Thornton, "(Un)equal Pay for Work of Equal Value," *Journal of Industrial Relations* 23 (Dec. 1981):471–72.

50. *National Wage and Equal Pay Cases 1972,* 147 Commonwealth Arbitration Reports 172, 178 (1972).

51. Thornton, "(Un)equal Pay," 466.

52. J.H. Porter, *Australian Compulsory Arbitration,* 2nd ed. (Sydney: Law Book Co., 1979), 39–40.

53. Ibid., 36.

54. Thornton, "(Un)equal Pay," 480.

55. 47 Book of Awards 1345.

56. For an account of the report of the Commission of Inquiry, see Nieuwenhuysen, "Equal Pay," 93–95.

57. Equal Pay Act of 1972, No. 118.

58. *Equal Pay Implementation in New Zealand* (Wellington: P.D. Hasselberg, 1979).

59. Theodore J. Schneyer, *Administrative Responsibility in Swedish Public Enterprise The Problem of Complex Goals* (Stockholm: Almqvist & Wiksell, 1970), 172.

60. Convention No. 100, printed in, International Labour Organisation, *International Labour Conventions and Recommendations 1971-1981* (Geneva: International Labour Office, 1982), 42–43.

61. Folke Schmidt, ed., *Discrimination in Employment* (Stockholm: Almqvist & Wiksell, 1978), 140.

62. SFS 1980:412. There is an English translation of the act in Gisbert H. Flanz,

Comparative Women's Rights and Political Participation in Europe (Dobbs Ferry, N.Y.: Transnational, 1983), 356–60.

63. For a general review of the act, see Reinhold Fahlbeck, *Labour Law in Sweden* (Lund, Sweden: Juridiska Föreningen, 1980), 54-55.

64. For a more detailed description of the bargaining structure in Sweden, see Folke Schmidt, "Labour Law" in *An Introduction to Swedish Law,* vol. 2, ed. Stig Strömholm (Deventer, The Netherlands: Kluwer, 1981), 279–301.

65. Gunnar Höogberg, "Recent Trends in Collective Bargaining in Sweden" in *Collective Bargaining in Industrialised Market Economies* (Geneva: International Labour Office, 1973), 351–52.

66. Bellace, "A Foreign Perspective," 160–61.

67. Alastair McAuley, *Women's Work and Wages in the Soviet Union* (London: George Allen & Unwin, 1981), 11.

Bibliography

Books and Articles

Akalin, Mustafa T. *Office Job Evaluation*. Des Plaines, Ill.: Industrial Management Society, 1970.

Arrow, Kenneth. "Models of Job Discrimination." In *Racial Discrimination in Economic Life,* edited by Anthony H. Pascal, 83–102. Lexington, Mass.: D.C. Heath, 1972.

———."The Theory of Discrimination." In *Discrimination in Labor Markets,* edited by Orley Ashenfelter and Albert Rees, 3–33. Princeton, N.J.: Princeton University Press, 1973.

Ashenfelter, Orley, and Rees, Albert. *Discrimination in Labor Markets*. Princeton, N.J.: Princeton University Press, 1973.

Assemblée Parlementaire Européenne, Débats, no. 46 (Oct. 20, 1961).

Barnes, David W. *Statistics as Proof*. Boston: Little, Brown, 1983.

Bayer, Alan E., and Astin, Helen S. "Sex Differences in Academic Rank and Salary Among Science Doctorates in Teaching." *Journal of Human Resources* 3 (spring 1968): 191–200.

Beatty, Richard W., and Beatty, James R. "Job Evaluation and Discrimination: Legal, Economic, and Measurement Perspectives on Comparable Worth and Women's Pay." In *Women in the Work Force,* edited by H. John Bernardin, 205–34. New York: Praeger, 1982.

———. "Some Problems with Contemporary Job Evaluation Systems." In *Comparable Worth and Wage Discrimination,* edited by Helen Remick, 59–78. Philadelphia: Temple University Press, 1984.

Becker, Gary S. *Economics of Discrimination,* 2nd ed. Chicago: The University of Chicago Press, 1971.

———. *Human Capital*. New York: Columbia University Press, 1964.

———. "Investment in Human Capital: A Theoretical Analysis." *Journal of Political Economy* 70 (Oct. 1962): 9–49.

———. "A Theory of the Allocation of Time." *The Economic Journal* 80 (Sept. 1965): 493–517.

Bellace, Janice R. "A Foreign Perspective." In *Comparable Worth: Issues and Alternatives,* edited by E. Robert Livernash, 137–72. Washington, D.C.: Equal Employment Advisory Council, 1980.

Blau, Francine D., and Jusenius, Carol L. "Economists' Approaches to Sex Segregation in the Labor Market: An Appraisal." In *Women and the Workplace,* edited by Martha Blaxall and Barbara Reagan, 181–99. Chicago: University of Chicago Press, 1976.

Blaxall, Martha and Reagan, Barbara, eds. *Women and the Workplace.* Chicago: University of Chicago Press, 1976.

Blinder, Alan S. "Wage Discrimination: Reduced Form and Structural Estimates." *Journal of Human Resources* 8 (fall 1973):436–55.

Blumrosen, Ruth G. "Wage Discrimination, Job Segregation, and Title VII of the Civil Rights Act of 1964." *University of Michigan Journal of Law Reform* 12 (spring 1979): 399–502.

Boothby, Daniel W. *The Determinants of Earnings and Occupation for Young Women.* New York: Garland, 1984.

Brown, Henry Phelps. *The Inequality of Pay.* Oxford: Oxford University Press, 1977.

Brown, Randall, S., Moon, Marilyn, and Zoloth, Barbara S. "Incorporating Occupational Attainment in Studies of Male-Female Earnings Differentials." *Journal of Human Resources* 15 (winter 1980):3–28.

Bureau of National Affairs. *Job Evaluation Policies & Procedures.* Washington, D.C.: Bureau of National Affairs, 1976.

Bureau of National Affairs. *Pay Equity and Comparable Worth.* Washington, D.C.: Bureau of National Affairs, 1984.

Cadieux, Rita. "Canada's Equal Pay for Work of Equal Value Law." In *Comparable Worth and Wage Discrimination,* edited by Helen Remick. Philadelphia: Temple University Press, 1984.

Carr, Shirley G.E. "Sex-Based Discrimination in Employment: Problems and Progress in Canada." *International Labour Review* 122 (Nov.-Dec. 1983):761–70.

Chiplin, Brian, and Sloane, Peter J. *Tackling Discrimination at the Workplace.* Cambridge: Cambridge University Press, 1982.

Clarke, Linda. "Equal Pay for Work of Equal Value." *New Law Journal* 134 (Feb. 1984):177.

———. "Proposed Amendments to the Equal Pay Act 1970—I." *New Law Journal* 133 (Oct. 1983):936.

———. "Proposed Amendments to the Equal Pay Act 1970—II." *New Law Journal* 133 (Dec. 1983): 1129–32.

Clifford, M. M., and Looft, W.R. "Academic Employment Interviews: Effect of Sex and Race." *Educational Research* 22 (1971):6–8.

Cocks, Sir Barnett. *The European Parliament.* London: Her Majesty's Stationery Office, 1973.

Cohen, Malcolm A. "Sex Differences in Compensation." *Journal of Human Resources* 6 (fall 1971):434–47.

Commission of the European Communities. *Community Law and Women.* Brussels: Commission of the European Communities, 1983.

Commission of the European Communities. *Report of the Commission to the Council on the Application as at 12 February 1978 of the Principle of Equal Pay for Men and Women,* COM (78)711. Brussels: Commission of the European Communities, 1979.

Commission Sociale. "Rapport intérimaire sur l'égalisation des salaires masculins et féminins." *Assemblée Parlementaire Européenne, Documents de Seance,* no. 68 (1961).

Corcoran, Mary E. "Work Experience, Labor Force Withdrawals, and Women's Wages: Empirical Results Using the 1976 Panel of Income Dynamics." In *Women in the Labor Market,* edited by Cynthia B. Lloyd, Emily S. Andrews, and Curtis L. Gilroy, 216–45. New York: Columbia University Press, 1979.

Corcoran, Mary, and Duncan, Greg J. "Work History, Labor Force Attachment, and Earnings Differences Between the Races and Sexes." *Journal of Human Resources* 14 (winter 1979):3–20.

"Council Directive of 10 February 1975 on the approximation of the laws of the Member States relating to the application of the principle of equal pay for men and women." *Official Journal of the European Communities* 18 (no. L 45 1975):19–20.

Dabscheck, Braham, and Niland, John. "Recent Trends in Collective Bargaining in Australia." *International Labour Review* 123 (Sept.-Oct. 1984):631–646.

Daymont, Thomas N., and Andrisani, Paul J. "Job Preferences, College Major, and the Gender Gap in Earnings." *Journal of Human Resources* 19 (summer 1984):408–28.

Deàn, Virginia, Roberts, Patti, and Boone, Carroll. "Comparable Worth Under Various Federal and State Laws." In *Comparable Worth and Wage Discrimination,* edited by Helen Remick, 238–266. Philadelphia: Temple University Press, 1984.

Department of Industrial Relations. *Australian Industrial Relations Systems.* Canberra: Australian Government Publishing Services, 1980.

Elizur, Dov. *Job Evaluation: A Systematic Approach.* Westmead, England: Gower, 1980.

Ely, John Hart. *Democracy and Distrust: A Theory of Judicial Review.* Cambridge, Mass.: Harvard University Press, 1980.

Equal Employment Advisory Council. *Comparable Worth: A Symposium on the Issues and Alternatives.* Washington, D.C.: Equal Employment Advisory Council, 1981.

Equal Pay Implementation in New Zealand. Wellington: P.D. Hasselberg, 1979.

Fahlbeck, Reinhold. *Labour Law in Sweden.* Lund, Sweden: Juridiska Föreningen, 1980.

Featherman, David L., and Hauser, Robert M. "Sexual Inequalities and Socio-Economic Achievement in the U.S., 1962–1973." *American Sociological Review* 41(June 1976):462–83.

Ferber, Marianne A., and Spaeth, Joe L. "Work Characteristics and the Male-Female Earnings Gap." *American Economic Review* 74 (May 1984):260–64.

Fidell, L.S. "Empirical Verification of Sex Discrimination in Hiring Practices." *American Psychologist* 25 (1970):1094–98.

Filer, Randall K. "Sexual Differences in Earnings: The Role of Individual Personalities and Tastes." *Journal of Human Resources* 18 (winter 1983):82–99.

Flanz, Gisbert H. *Comparative Women's Rights and Political Participation in Europe.* Dobbs Ferry, N.Y.: Transnational, 1983.

Fuchs, Victor R. "Differences in Hourly Earnings Between Men and Women." *Monthly Labor Review* 94 (May 1971):9–15.

Galanter, Marc. "Reading the Landscape of Disputes: What We Know and Don't

Know (and Think We Know) About Our Allegedly Contentious and Litigious Society." *UCLA Law Review* 31 (Oct. 1983):4–71.

General Accounting Office. *Options for Conducting a Pay Equity Study of Federal Pay and Classification Systems.* Washington, D.C.: U.S. Government Printing Office, 1985.

Gold, Michael Evan. *A Dialogue on Comparable Worth.* Ithaca, N.Y.: ILR Press, 1983.

Goldberger, Arthur S. "Reverse Regression and Salary Discrimination." *Journal of Human Resources* 19 (summer 1984):293–318.

Gordon, David M. "Economic Dimensions of Occupational Segregation—Comment II." In *Women and the Workplace,* edited by Martha Blaxall and Barbara Reagan, 238–44. Chicago: University of Chicago Press, 1976.

Gordon, Nancy M., Morton, Thomas E., and Braden, Ina C. "Faculty Salaries: Is There Discrimination by Sex, Race, and Discipline?" *American Economic Review* 64 (June 1974):419–27.

Green, Carole A., and Ferber, Marianne A. "Employment Discrimination: An Empirical Test of Forward Versus Reverse Regression." *Journal of Human Resources* 19 (fall 1984):557–69.

Gwartney, James, and Stroup, Richard. "Measurement of Employment Discrimination According to Sex." *Southern Economic Journal* 39 (April 1973):575–87.

Hildebrand, George. "The Market System." In *Comparable Worth: Issues and Alternatives,* edited by E. Robert Livernash, 79–106. Washington: Equal Employment Advisory Council, 1980.

Hirsch, Barry T., and Leppel, Karen, "Sex Discrimination in Faculty Salaries: Evidence from a Historically Women's University." *American Economic Review* 72 (Sept. 1982):829–35.

Hoffman, Carl C., Quade, Dana. "Regression and Discrimination." *Sociological Methods & Research* 11 (May 1983):407–42.

Höogberg, Gunnar. "Recent Trends in Collective Bargaining in Sweden." In *Collective Bargaining in Industrialised Market Economies,* 337–52. Geneva: International Labour Office, 1973.

Horowitz, Stanley A., and Sherman, Allan. "A Direct Measure of the Relationship Between Human Capital and Productivity." *Journal of Human Resources* 15 (winter 1980):67–76.

International Labour Office. *Women at Work,* no. 1. Geneva: International Labour Office, 1983.

———. *Yearbook of Labour Statistics.* Geneva: International Labour Office, 1984.

International Labour Organisation. *International Labour Conventions and Recommendations 1919–1981.* Geneva: International Labour Office, 1982.

———. *International Labour Conventions and Recommdations 1971–1981.* Geneva: International Labour Office, 1982.

———. *Job Evaluation.* Geneva: International Labour Office, 1960.

Johnson, George E., and Stafford, Frank P. "The Earnings and Promotion of Women Faculty." *American Economic Review* 64 (Dec. 1974):888–903.

Landau, C.E. "Recent Legislation and Case Law in the EEC on Sex Equality in Employment." *International Labour Review* 123 (Jan.-Feb. 1984):53–70.

Landes, Elisabeth M. "Sex Differences in Wages and Employment: A Test of the Specific Capital Hypothesis." *Economic Inquiry* 15 (Oct. 1977):523–38.

Lanham, Elizabeth. *Job Evaluation.* New York: McGraw-Hill, 1955.

Livernash, E. Robert, ed. *Comparable Worth: Issues and Alternatives.* Washington, D.C.: Equal Employment Advisory Council, 1980.

Livy, Bryan. *Job Evaluation: A Critical Review.* New York: John Wiley, 1975.

Lloyd, Cynthia B., Andrews, Emily S., and Gilroy, Curtis L., eds. *Women in the Labor Market.* New York: Columbia University Press, 1979.

Lloyd, Cynthia B., and Niemi, Beth T. *The Economics of Sex Differentials.* New York: Columbia University Press, 1979.

McAuley, Alastair. *Women's Work and Wages in the Soviet Union.* London: George Allen & Unwin, 1981.

Malkiel, Burton G., and Malkiel, Judith A. "Male-Female Pay Differentials in Professional Employment." *American Economic Review* 63 (Sept. 1973):693–705.

Maranto, Cheryl L., and Rodgers, Robert C. "Does Work Experience Increase Productivity? A Test of the On-the-Job Training Hypothesis." *Journal of Human Resources* 19 (summer 1984):341–57.

Mellor, Earl F. "Investigating the Differences in Weekly Earnings of Women and Men." *Monthly Labor Review* 107 (June 1984):17–28.

Mincer, Jacob, and Polachek, Solomon. "Family Investments in Human Capital: Earnings of Women." *Journal of Political Economy* 82 (March/April 1974):S76–S108.

Nieuwenhuysen, John, and Hicks, John. "Equal Pay for Women in Australia and New Zealand." In *Equal Pay for Women,* edited by Barrie O. Pettman, 63–97. Bradford, England: MCB Books, 1975.

Niland, John. *Collective Bargaining and Compulsory Arbitration in Australia.* Kensington, Australia: New South Wales University Press, 1978.

Oaxaca, Ronald. "Male-Female Wage Differentials in Urban Labor markets." *International Economic Review* 14 (Oct. 1973):693–709.

Office for the Official Publications of the European Communities, *Treaties Establishing the European Communities.* Luxembourg: Office for the Official Publications of the European Communities, 1973.

Pascal, Anthony H., ed. *Racial Discrimination in Economic Life.* Lexington, Mass.: D.C. Heath, 1972.

Perlman, M. *Judges in Industry: A Study of Labour Arbitration in Australia.* Melbourne: Melbourne University Press, 1954.

Pheterson, G.I., Kiesler, S.B., and Goldberg, P.A. "Evaluation of the Performance of Women as a Function of Their Sex, Achievement, and Personal History." *Journal of Personality and Social Psychology* 19 (1971):114–18.

Piore, Michael J., ed. *Unemployment and Inflation.* White Plains, N.Y.: M.E. Sharpe, 1979.

Porter, J. H. *Australian Compulsory Arbitration,* 2nd ed. Sydney: Law Book Co., 1979.

Ragan, James F., Jr., and Smith, Sharon P. "The Impact of Differences in Turnover Rates on Male/Female Pay Differentials." *Journal of Human Resources* 16 (summer 1981):343–65.

Remick, Helen, ed. *Comparable Worth and Wage Discrimination.* Philadelphia: Temple University Press, 1984.

Remick, Helen. "Major Issues in *a priori* Applications." In *Comparable Worth and Wage Discrimination,* edited by Helen Remick, 99–117. Philadelphia: Temple University Press, 1984.

Remus, William E., and Kelly, Lane. "Evidence of Sex Discrimination: In Similar Populations, Men Are Paid Better Than Women." *American Journal of Economics and Sociology* 42 (April 1983):149–52.

Robinson, Joan. "What is Perfect Competition?" *The Quarterly Journal of Economics* (Nov. 1934):104–20.

Ronalds, Chris. *Anti-Discrimination Legislation in Australia.* Sydney: Butterworth, 1979.

Roos, Patricia A. "Sex Stratification in the Workplace: Male-Female Differences in Economic Returns to Occupation." *Social Science Research* 10 (March 1981):195–224.

Rosen, Benson, and Jerdee, Thomas H. "Effects of Applicant's Sex and Difficulty of Job on Evaluations of Candidates for Managerial Positions." *Journal of Applied Psychology* 59 (Aug. 1974):511–12.

———. "Influence of Sex Role Stereotypes on Personnel Decisions." *Journal of Applied Psychology* 59 (Feb. 1974):9–14.

———. "Sex Stereotyping in the Executive Suite." *Harvard Business Review* 52 (March-April 1974):45–58.

Rytina, Nancy F. "Earnings of Men and Women: A Look at Specific Occupations." *Monthly Labor Review* 105 (April 1982):25–31.

———. "Tenure as a Factor in the Male-Female Earnings Gap." *Monthly Labor Review* 105 (April 1982):32–34.

Sanborn, Henry. "Pay Differences Between Men and Women." *Industrial and Labor Relations Review* 17 (July 1964):534–50.

Sandell, Steven H., and Shapiro, David. "A Reexamination of the Evidence." *Journal of Human Resources* 8 (winter 1978):103–17.

Sawhill, Isabel V. "The Economics of Discrimination Against Women: Some New Findings." *Journal of Human Resources* 8 (summer 1973):383–96.

Schmidt, Folke, ed. *Discrimination in Employment.* Stockholm: Almqvist & Wiksell, 1978.

Schmidt, Folke. "Labour Law." In *An Introduction to Swedish Law,* vol. 2, edited by Stig Strömholm, 279–301. Deventer, The Netherlands: Kluwer, 1981.

Schneyer, Theodore J. *Administrative Responsibility in Swedish Public Enterprise The Problem of Complex Goals.* Stockholm: Almqvist & Wiksell, 1970.

Schwab, Donald P. "Job Evaluation and Pay Setting: Concepts and Practices." In *Comparable Worth: Issues and Alternatives,* edited by E. Robert Livernash, 49–77. Washington, D.C.: Equal Employment Advisory Council, 1980.

Schwab, Donald P., and Wichern, Dean W. "Systematic Bias in Job Evaluation and Market Wages: Implications for the Comparable Worth Debate." *Journal of Applied Psychology* 68 (Feb. 1983):60–69.

Smith, James P., and Ward, Michael P. *Women's Wages and Work in the Twentieth Century.* Santa Monica, Calif.: The Rand Corp., 1984.

Stanley, Julian C., and Hopkins, Kenneth D. *Educational and Psychological Measurement and Evaluation.* Englewood Cliffs, N.J.: Prentice-Hall, 1972.

Statistics Canada, Social and Economic Studies Division. *Women in Canada A Statistical Report.* Ottawa: Minister of Supply & Services Canada, 1985.

Stonier, Alfred W., and Hague, Douglas C. *A Textbook of Economic Theory,* 5th ed. London: Longman, 1980.

Sullivan, Charles A., Zimmer, Michael J., and Richards, Richard F. *Federal Statutory*

Law of Employment Discrimination. Indianapolis: The Michie Co., 1980.

Tarnopolsky, Walter Surma. *Discrimination and the Law in Canada.* Toronto: Richard De Boo, 1982.

Thornton, Margaret. "(Un)Equal Pay for Work of Equal Value." *Journal of Industrial Relations* 23 (Dec. 1981):466–81.

Thurow, Lester. *Generating Inequality.* New York: Basic Books, 1975.

Treiman, Donald J. "Effect of Choice of Factors and Factor Weights in Job Evaluation." In *Comparable Worth and Wage Discrimination,* edited by Helen Remick, 79–89. Philadelphia: Temple University Press, 1984.

———. *Job Evaluation: An Analytic Review.* Washington, D.C.: National Academy of Sciences, 1979.

Treiman, Donald J., and Hartmann, Heidi I. *Women, Work, and Wages: Equal Pay for Jobs of Equal Value.* Washington, D.C.: National Academy Press, 1981.

Treiman, Donald J., Hartmann, Heidi I., and Roos, Patricia A. "Assessing Pay Discrimination Using National Data." In *Comparable Worth and Wage Discrimination,* edited by Helen Remick, 137–54. Philadelphia: Temple University Press, 1984.

Tsuchigane, Robert, and Dodge, Norton. *Economic Discrimination Against Women in the United States.* Lexington, Mass.: D.C. Heath, 1974.

U.S. Bureau of the Census. *1980 Census of Population, Subject Reports, Earnings by Occupation and Education.* Washington, D.C.: U.S. Government Printing Office, 1984.

U.S. Commission on Civil Rights. *Comparable Worth: Issue for the 80's,* 2 vols. Washington, D.C.: U.S. Government Printing Office, 1984.

U.S. Department of Labor, Women's Bureau. *Time of Change: 1983 Handbook on Women Workers.* Washington, D.C.: U.S. Government Printing Office, 1983.

Walster, Elaine, Cleary, T. Anne, and Clifford, Margaret M. "Research Note: The Effect of Race and Sex on College Admission." *Sociology of Education* 41 (spring 1970):237–44.

Willborn, Steven L. "The Disparate Impact Model of Discrimination: Theory and Limits." *American University Law Review* 34, no. 3 (1985):799–837.

Witt, Mary, and Naherny, Patricia K. *Women's Work: Up From .878.* Madison: University of Wisconsin-Extension, 1975.

Zimmer, Michael J., Sullivan, Charles A., and Richards, Richard F. *Cases and Materials on Employment Discrimination.* Boston: Little, Brown, 1982.

Cases

AFSCME v. State of Washington, 578 F. Supp. 846 (W.D. Wash. 1983), *rev'd,* 770 F.2d 1401 (9th Cir. 1985).

Albemarle Paper Co. v. Moody, 422 U.S. 405, 425 (1975).

American Nurses Ass'n v. State of Illinois, 37 FEP Cases 705 (N.D. Ill. 1985).

Basic Wage Inquiry of 1949–50, 68 Commonwealth Arbitration Reports 698 (1949).

Briggs v. City of Madison, 536 F. Supp. 435 (W.D. Wis. 1982).

Christensen v. Iowa, 563 F.2d 353 (8th Cir. 1977).

Clothing Trades Award of 1919, 13 Commonwealth Arbitration Reports 647 (1919).

La Commission des Broits de la Personne du Quebec v. La Ferme de la Poulette Grise, Inc., 3 Canadian Human Rights Reporter paras. 6235–6249 (1982).

Commission of the European Communities v. United Kingdom of Great Britain and Northern Ireland, [1982] I.R.L.R. 333 (European Court of Justice).

Commonwealth v. Tasmania, 46 Australian Law Reports 625 (1983).

EEOC v. Federal Reserve Bank, 698 F.2d 633 (4th Cir. 1983).

Equal Pay Cases, 127 Commonwealth Arbitration Reports 1142 (1969).

Francoeur v. Corroon & Black Co., 552 F. Supp. 403 (S.D.N.Y. 1982).

Fruit Packers' Case, 6 Commonwealth Arbitration Reports 61 (1912).

Furnco Construction Co. v. Waters, 438 U.S. 567 (1978).

Gerlach v. Michigan Bell Telephone Co., 501 F. Supp. 1300 (E.D. Mich. 1980).

Harris v. Ford Motor Co., 26 E.P.D. para. 31,906 (8th Cir. 1981).

Hayward v. Cammell Laird Shipbuilders Ltd., [1984] I.R.L.R. 463 (Industrial Tribunal).

International Union of Electrical Workers v. Westinghouse Electric Corp., 631 F.2d 1094 (3d Cir. 1980), *cert. denied,* (452 U.S. 967 1981).

Lemons v. City and County of Denver, 620 F.2d 228 (10th Cir.), *cert. denied,* 449 U.S. 888 (1980).

Los Angeles Department of Water & Power v. Manhart, 435 U.S. 702 (1978).

McDonnell Douglas v. Green, 411 U.S. 792 (1973).

National Wage and Equal Pay Cases 1972, 147 Commonwealth Arbitration Reports 172 (1972).

O'Brien v. Sim-Chem Limited, [1980] I.R.L.R. 373 (House of Lords).

Peques v. Mississippi State Employment Service, 699 F.2d 760 (5th Cir. 1983).

Public Service Alliance of Canada v. Treasury Board, unreported.

Spaulding v. University of Washington, 740 F.2d 686 (9th Cir.), *cert. denied,* 105 S.Ct. 511 (1984).

Statutes

United States Statutes

Equal Pay Act of 1963, 29 U.S.C. sec. 206(d) (1982).

Title VII of the Civil Rights Act of 1964, 42 U.S.C. secs. 2000e to 2000e–17 (1982).

State Laws

Alaska Stat. sec. 18.80.220 (1984).

Ark. Stat. Ann. sec. 81–624 (1976).

Ark. Stat. Ann. sec. 81–333 (Supp. 1983).

Ga. Code Ann. secs. 54–1001, 54-1003 (1982 & Supp. 1982).

Idaho Code sec. 44–1702(1) (1977).

Ky. Rev. Stat. sec. 337.423(1) (1981).

Me. Rev. Stat. Ann. tit. 26, sec. 628 (Supp. 1984–85).

Md. Ann. Code art. 100, sec. 55A (1979).

Mass. Gen. Laws Ann. ch. 149, sec. 105A (West 1982).

Minn. Stat. sec. 43A(3) (1982).

Neb. Rev. Stat. secs. 48–1219, 48–1221 (1984).

N.D. Cent. Code sec. 34–06.1–03 (1980).

Okla Stat. Ann. tit. 40, sec. 198.1 (Supp. 1984–85).

Or. Rev. Stat. sec. 652.220 (1983).

Pa. Stat. Ann. tit. 43, sec. 336.3 (Purdon Supp. 1984).

S.D. Codified Laws sec. 60–12–15 (1978).

Tenn. Code Ann. sec. 50–2–202(a) (1983).

Tex. Stat. Ann. tit. 117, art. 6825 (Vernon 1960).

W. Va. Code sec. 21–5B–3 (1981).

Foreign Statutes

Act on Equal Opportunities for Women and Men at Work, SFS 1980:412 (Sweden).

Canadian Human Rights Act (1977) (Canada).

The Equal Pay Act, 1970, ch. 41, as amended (United Kingdom).

Equal Pay Act of 1972, No. 118 (New Zealand).

Quebec Charter of Human Rights and Freedoms, Section 19, R.S.Q. 1977, c. C–12. as amended (Canada).

Sex Discrimination Act 1984, No. 4 (Australia).

Index

Kelly, L., 23, 24
Kiesler, S.B., 104*n*.25

*La Commission des Broits de la
Personne du Quebec v. La Ferme de
la Poulette Grise, Inc.*, 86–87
Labor market: dual model, 28–29;
external vs. internal, 27–28,
101*n*.27; human capital theory of
value in, 11; influence on value of
job, 4–5; structure of, 27–29; wage
disparities based on demand in, 47–
49, 51, 52–53, 54, 56–57
Labor relations, Swedish, 94–95. *See
also* Unions
Labor, division of, 26
Landau, C.E., 106*n*.8
Landes, E.M., 21, 23
Lanham, E., 103*n*.11
Legal setting for litigation, 33–34
Legislation, comparable worth, 59–75,
105*n*.44; in Australia, 87–90; in
Canada, 85–87; data collection for,
60–61; in European Economic
Community, 79–85; federal, 75;
implementation of, 67–70; job
evaluation for, 61–67; level of proof
required to warrant, 67; in New
Zealand, 90–93; private, 75; for
private employers, 70–74; for public
employees, 59–70; in Sweden, 93–
95
Leppel, K., 22, 24
Litigation, comparable worth, 33–58;
Briggs v. City of Madison, 42–51,
61, 71; in Canada, 87; common
understanding of comparable worth
from, 3–4; comparable worth
studies and likelihood of, 60–61,
70; complexity of, 58; costs of, 57–
58; *County of Washington v.
Gunther*, 35–41; disparate impact
discrimination and, 41, 51–57;
disparate treatment discrimination
and, 41–51; employment
discrimination theories and, 41–57;
failure to test state laws through,
74; legal setting for, 33–34;
shortcomings of, 57–58; *Spaulding
v. University of Washington*, 52–57;
theoretical limitations, 58

Livernash, E.R., 101*n*.33
Lloyd, C.B., 100*n*.15
LO (Swedish Confederation of Trade
Unions), 94
Local Government Pay Equity Act
(Minnesota), 69–70
Looft, W.R., 104*n*.25
*Los Angeles Dept. of Water & Power
v. Manhart*, 39–40
"Low wage" claims in Sweden, 95
Luxembourg. *See* European Economic
Community (EEC)

McAuley, A., 109*n*.67
Maine, comparable worth laws in, 72–
73
Malkiel, B.G., 23, 24, 99*n*.5
Malkiel, J.A., 23, 24, 99*n*.5
Maranto, C.L., 100*n*.11
Market. *See* Labor market
Maryland, comparable worth laws in:
applicable to private sector
employers in, 72–73;
implementation plan for, 67–68
Massachusetts, comparable worth laws
in, 60, 72–73, 74
Mellor, E.F., 14, 15, 21, 23
Merit as affirmative defense, 72, 74
Mincer, J., 14, 15, 100*n*.15, 101*n*.23
Minimum Wage Act (1945) (New
Zealand), 91
Minnesota Legislative Commission on
Employee Relations, 68, 69
Minnesota, comparable worth laws in,
68–70, 75
Moon, M., 20, 23
Motte, M., 106*n*.4
Multicollinearity, 16
Multiple regression analysis, 11, 12–16

Naherny, P.K., 104*n*.27
Nebraska, comparable worth laws in,
72–73
Neimi, B.T., 100*n*.15
Neoclassical economics, 10, 99*n*.7
Neoclassical human capital approach,
101*n*.27
Netherlands. *See* European Economic
Community (EEC)
New Mexico, implementation plan for
comparable worth in, 67–68

About the Author

Steven L. Willborn is professor of law at the University of Nebraska–Lincoln. He was educated at Northland College (B.A., 1974) and the University of Wisconsin–Madison (M.S., J.D., 1976). From 1976–1979, Mr. Willborn was a lawyer in private practice in Cleveland, Ohio. In 1979, he joined the faculty at the University of Nebraska. During the 1985–1986 academic year, Mr. Willborn was on leave from the university, as a Fulbright Scholar conducting research at the Institute of Advanced Legal Studies in London. Mr. Willborn has been licensed to practice law in Nebraska, Ohio, and Wisconsin and to make cheese in Wisconsin. He has written numerous articles on labor and employment discrimination law.